THE STORY OF

CHANNON

ROSE

PART II

by

CHANNON ROSE

Legal Disclaimer

This book
is dedicated to my
damn self!

Most people dedicate their books to a loved one or someone special who helped them along the way in life. Instead, I am going to dedicate this book TO MY DAMN SELF! That might sound selfish or off-putting, but let me explain. During this time in my life, I didn't have someone helping me out along the way. I was a "bad kid" and my parents weren't jumping at the opportunity to pay for my college or rent. I don't blame them. Why would they? They also knew I received settlement money from my car accident when I turned 18 so they thought I was fine financially. They didn't know I spent ALL the money in only four months. I was too scared to tell them or ask for help, so I had to rely on myself. I believe when you are an adult you should do that anyway. I never wanted to depend on my parents, so I always found ways to support myself, but they weren't always "acceptable" or what people would call traditional means.

At first, I hid my secret life in porn because I was scared of what others might think. I was afraid of being judged or people telling me I shouldn't do what I was doing. I also thought anyone telling me this wasn't going to be the one paying for me to go to school, or pay my rent or bills. I was out there doing what I needed to do to get through life the best way I knew how. For these reasons, I think it is fitting for this book to be dedicated to me, because I am all I had at the time. Besides, I doubt anyone I know wants to be recognized in a book all about my life in porn and escorting.

Oh wait... I almost forgot. I would also like to dedicate this book to all the people I escorted for who never chopped me up into a million pieces. Okay, that is all.

TABLE OF CONTENTS

THE STORY OF CHANNON ROSE

INTRODUCTION

First and foremost, I would like to thank you for purchasing this book. Yes, YOU. The one reading this right now. Thank you. Thank you for supporting me and allowing me to share my story with you. It really means a lot and I want you to know how grateful I am. Without YOU, I would not be where I am today. With that said, let me take a step back and say hi! Most of you know me as Channon Rose; some of you know me as Randi Wright, and some of you may even know me as Goddess Randi. If you don't know all three, don't worry, you will soon.

I might be a little different from people who prefer to shut out or bottle up their past, especially if their past involved doing porn, fetish work, escorting and or being a stripper. I on the other hand, embrace who I am and who I was. Who we once were does not always reflect who we might be today. The choices I made were my own and provided an amazing time in my life for many years. Our past is a part of our own individual story and we should accept it whether it was good or bad. Please don't view the phrase, "Accept it," in a negative way, but one of growth and a part of life. I say this because nobody's perfect, and no two lives are the same. My choices in life may not be right for you, and vice versa. It is, after all, my life and my journey, just as you have your own life and your own journey. We're all different and special in our own way and have our own directions in life. There are good times and bad times, and sometimes we stumble and fall but we always get back up! I believe life is a learning lesson and we should always be learning and growing along the way.

I've had a lot of fun in my life and I still do, but in this book I detail a very wild and crazy specific time of my life that I wouldn't trade for anything. To say it was an awesome time filled with travel, money, and once-in-a-lifetime experiences would be an understatement. I was involved in the adult entertainment industry for close to a decade and this book recounts my life during that time. So how did I get there and where did it all begin?

In my first book *The Story of Channon Rose – Lessons Between the Lines* I wrote about the difficulties and struggles I went through as a child and teenager. If you've read it, then you know there were many! *The Story of Channon Rose – Lessons Between the Lines* was the first book in this series and it captured my life from birth until 18 years old. If you haven't read my first book, I encourage you to read it if possible, as it provides a foundation and background to this book. However, the first sentence in Chapter 1 of this book, I share the final moments of my first book to provide you with a seamless transition into this one. *The Story of Channon Rose - Part II* is the second installment in my series, and it picks up where my first book left off. Thank you again and enjoy!

How It All Began

"If you are unwilling to risk the unusual, you will have to settle for the ordinary."

- Jim Rohn

Excerpt taken from my first book *The Story of Channon Rose*
– Lessons Between the Lines

I spent four months dancing at that strip club until one night something happened that would change my life forever.

I was now a STRIPPER! It took me a while to learn the ropes as a stripper, considering I had just turned 18 and had never stepped foot in a strip club in my life. It seems silly, but until you're working your first day as a stripper, you really don't know what to do other than dance on the stage; but that is not all a stripper does! Most of the money you make as a stripper comes from private lap dances, but I didn't even know lap dances happened at strip clubs until my first day on the job. I had so much to learn and I was so nervous. I soon found a quick fix for that: alcohol. Vodka to be exact. You might be wondering how I drank on the job. I was crafty, often pouring it into water bottles that I took into work. I had to learn what to wear, how to dance, how to ask guys for a lap dance and I was a total AMATEUR. After a few days on the job, I caught on and to be honest, it was really fun for me.

Backstage my first month as a stripper (18 years old)

"I don't care about anyone not liking me. Bitches barely like themselves."

- Cardi B
(Ex-stripper, now successful rapper)

An average day for me as a stripper went something like this: I would wake up hungover around 1pm and smoke a cigarette in bed. When I finally found the motivation to actually get out of bed, I'd head to the bathroom to brush my teeth, wash my face and throw my hair in a messy bun without even brushing it. I would put on some oversized black sunglasses and leave the house in my pajamas that is left in because I

12

was too lazy to put real clothes on. Having to get all made up every night for work made me never want to "get ready" when I wasn't working, so when I went out I gave zero fucks about my appearance.

I would walk out the door looking like a hot mess to run errands, like getting cigarettes, vodka, chips, bottled water and Kit Kats from 7/11, and if time permitted, do some shopping. When I say shopping, I don't mean grocery shopping, I mean shopping for clothes, shoes, and purses. It wasn't all useless spending, as I did buy some new outfits for work. It just so happened that my work clothes were pretty interesting and fun. My work attire was definitely different than your average woman's corporate pantsuit or cardigan. The stripper "dress code" is a little more scandalous. Think, see-through panties, lacy bras, and tight, short skirts. Sometimes we wore costumes like schoolgirl outfits and naughty nurses costumes. Anything you think of as a slutty Halloween costume, I probably wore at some point, but we would just make the outfits EXTRA slutty. The whole point was to wear something that would get the customer's attention and make them willing to spend their money on us.

Okay, back to the schedule. At some point in the day, my hunger would kick in or someone would remind me that I should probably eat. Cigarettes suppressed my appetite, so I rarely ate breakfast. I just wasn't hungry. I would smoke cigarettes for breakfast and then down some water because I was so thirsty and dehydrated from drinking so much alcohol the night before. Typically by the afternoon I was hungry again. Fortunately, I knew the location of every Taco Bell in the San Fernando Valley. Taco Bell was my favorite! I would go through the drive thru and order the same thing every time: two steak tacos with extra cheese, extra white sauce, and a small Sierra Mist. I had no idea what the white sauce was but it was delicious and I wanted a lot of it on my tacos. That meal would usually last me throughout the day. I would eat one taco in the car on the way home, and the other one I would throw in the fridge and heat up later that night. I basically lived on Taco Bell, cigarettes and vodka.

At this point, I was living with my boyfriend Joe and his friend Brian. Joe was tall, had spiky brown hair, brown eyes, and was super hot. When I got home one night from working at the strip club, I saw they were smoking weed on our balcony, which was a common occurrence even though smoking weed was illegal then. All my boyfriend did was smoke pot. Joe didn't have a job and was living off of me. It began to annoy me that I spent majority of my time working and going to school full-time and he stayed home all day smoking. I just didn't think it was fair. The only money coming in during that time was from my job at the strip club. I'm sure Joe or Brian had no intention of getting a job, probably because I was paying for both of their lifestyles and so they must have thought they didn't need one. I had to pay all of our bills, rent, food, normal expenses, and on top of that, Joe's $100 a day marijuana habit. I was a SUCKER.

I became so fed up with him not working that I asked my dad to offer Joe a job. My dad owned his own electrical company and was nice enough to give him a job. Not long after Joe started working for my dad, my dad told me to me that he didn't like Joe. He said Joe was lazy, smoked weed on the job (which could have been a huge liability in itself), and basically thought Joe was a loser. For obvious reasons, Joe working for my dad didn't last long. My boyfriend ultimately didn't really want to work. He lacked drive and motivation to make money, while I was busting my naked ass in a strip club every night not only to pay for my own stuff, but his too.

Unfortunately, I was so in love with him that I didn't see his manipulation. I didn't know at the time that Joe did not like that I worked at a strip club, which is ironic since he was the one to suggest I dance there in the first place. He never mentioned his feelings to me, so I'm not sure why he felt the way he did. He might have been jealous of the money I was making or uncomfortable with other men/women seeing me naked, which is completely understandable, but none of that was brought up. In any relationship, communication is essential and if you don't have it, resentment and problems grow quickly. I'm not sure why he never flat-out asked me to stop dancing or admitted he wasn't happy with it. However, being only 18 and going to school full time, stripping was probably the highest-paying legal job that I was going to get. If I was going to pay our bills, rent, and everything else I had to keep stripping and I think he knew that, which is most likely why he kept quiet. Needless to say, our relationship started to go downhill.

One day, after working at the strip club for about two months, I came home as usual from school for the day. I got ready for work and kissed Joe goodbye since by the time I would get home from work it was late and he was sleeping. When I got home later that night, it was anything but normal. Something was way off as soon as I walked in the door.

From the front door of our apartment, I noticed that all of the pictures of Joe and me in the apartment were missing. I didn't think a burglar would want random pictures of me, so I was kind of freaked out; I had to check to make sure I was in the right apartment. My art supplies and my fashion design books were missing too. More and more things were missing as I looked around. I walked into our bedroom and Joe was in our bed sleeping as usual. I woke him up to ask him about the missing items, but as soon as he woke up, I could tell he was drunk and high. He was mumbling and stumbling on his own words. I could tell that he hadn't been asleep for very long. He explained that he was the one who had moved my things. One positive thing about Joe is that he was brutally honest. He slowly and hesitantly responded that he had a girl over at our apartment and hid my things to hide that he had a girlfriend.

I instantly became furious. Any girlfriend would be. I felt as though he didn't even try to hide the fact that he was cheating on me and I wondered how long this had been going on. At least put my shit back on the walls, you idiot! Joe and I had an off-and-on relationship and to be honest, this wasn't the first time he cheated on me. I'll take part of the blame for trusting him again, but it sucked either way. I ended up kicking his loser ass out of the apartment that night. I finally had enough. I was now single and on my own, a stripper and a full-time college student. Look out world!

"Always go with the choice that scares you the most, because that is what is going to help you grow." - Caroline Myss

I continued dancing after my breakup with Joe. Some of the girls hated stripping, but I loved it. It felt good to be bad. I liked the idea of doing something that was considered bad. For me, it was exciting. For the most part, you have two kinds of strip clubs: clubs that are 18 and over and the strippers are fully nude. The other kind of strip club admits anyone over 21, and they serve alcohol but the strippers are only topless and cannot be fully nude.

I worked at an all-nude 18 and over strip club in the San Fernando Valley in Southern California. Some strippers move around a bit between different strip clubs but I stayed at the same one because I felt most comfortable there and strippers can be super mean to new girls. When you become a stripper, you're encouraged to pick a stage name for safety reasons, and I of course picked the most embarrassing and lame stripper name. My stage name was Star. At the time, I thought it was cool. You also got to pick your own music to dance to on stage and I would usually dance to "The Beautiful People" by Marilyn Manson or "Cherry Pie" by Warrant. You know, the usual stripper songs.

Me at the strip club in one of my stripper outfits (18 years old)

A lot goes on behind the scenes as a stripper that many people may assume but don't know for sure. I will tell you about my experience. Backstage there was a dressing room where all the strippers got ready or hung out when they weren't on the floor or stage. This is where they could touch up their makeup or change their outfits. A majority of the girls were on some combination of drugs or alcohol, though they all had their sneaky ways of hiding it. Mine was pouring my vodka into a water bottle. Others hid their meth, coke, or another drug of choice in their lockers or up their butt (not joking) and then secretly take it to a bathroom stall to get high at work.

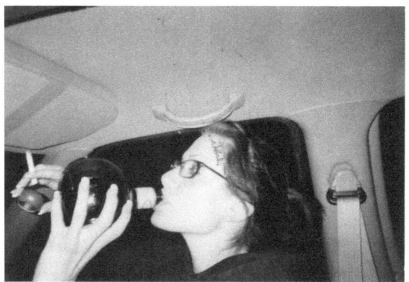

Rare occasion of me drinking something other than vodka (In someone's car at the club drinking on my break)

The girls had their cliques and could be really catty with each other, though I tried to steer clear of that as much as I could. It was hard because new girls tend to get a lot of attention at clubs, especially with regulars, and the veteran strippers didn't like us taking away their business. Also, most of the strippers weren't the type of girls you could trust. Some girls would steal from other ones, so they all had these little caboodle boxes they would take with them on stage and to their private lap dances. The boxes held their valuables, including money they made that night, lip-gloss, cellphone, and I am sure their drugs.

When you first become a stripper, it feels intimidating and you are self-conscious of your dancing, but after awhile you get used to it and then it becomes more competitive. You are there to make money and that is what is on your mind. I didn't see stripping as a bad thing like so many other people do. I think I've always been more comfortable with things that other people aren't. Sure I got drunk a lot when I went to work, partially because it gave me confidence as alcohol does for most people, but also because it was fun to drink. I liked the way alcohol made me feel. I was 18 and this was the time in my life I was supposed to be partying. Other girls may have been getting drunk at college parties but I was just doing life a little differently and getting drunk and partying in a strip club instead. It also was a bonus that I was making money while I was at it.

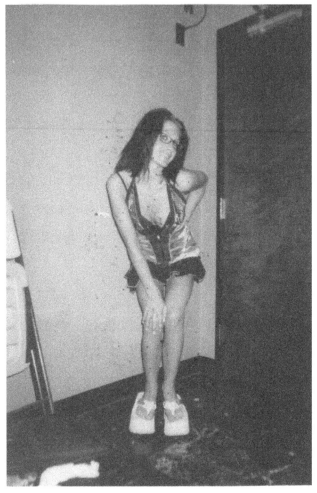

Me at the strip club wearing platform sandals instead of stripper heals (So embarrassing)

Another month or so went by and it was a typical night in the strip club, or so I thought. I was walking around in the club trying to find someone to give a lap dance to when a tall, well-dressed, overweight man who looked to be in his mid-thirties stopped me. I had never seen this man before. He asked me if I had a minute to talk with him. I sat down next to him, expecting him to ask me how much it was for a private dance.

Instead, he asked if I had ever been interested in nude modeling. I didn't know if he was a photographer or an agent, but I didn't have to think twice about answering his question. After all, let's get real here: I'm naked on stage every night! Nude modeling seemed fun and something I would feel comfortable doing. I replied, "Sure I can do that!" He smiled and handed me his business card and told me to call him so we could set up a meeting. I was barely 18 years old and still new to the adult world. I was naive and never once thought that this guy may try to get in my pants or may be a stripper serial killer who wanted to have sex with me and then chop me into a million pieces. I legitimately thought a modeling agency was interested in signing me.

I was so excited that I called him first thing the next morning. After we talked on the phone, we set up a time to meet with the agency. The meeting was scheduled for two days later! I was so excited about my meeting and possibly a modeling opportunity. I had always wanted to be a model but unfortunately, my genetics weren't typical model material. I'm only 5'3", which is short in general, but extremely short in the modeling world. I wasn't tall enough and at the time & I thought my looks were just okay. The fact that I even had a chance to meet with an agency was a dream come true.

The wait over the next two days felt like it took forever but then the day finally arrived. I was meeting with a modeling agency today. I didn't know it at the time but walking into the office that day would change my life forever. I was beyond excited and I spent the morning planning my outfit. I wanted every little detail to be just right. After all, this was my big day. I spent extra time on my hair and makeup and wanted to dress extra cute to impress the agents. I decided to wear my hair straight down and do a full face of makeup, which isn't typical, but I didn't know that. In the modeling world, you don't wear makeup to meet with agents and if you do it is very minimal; but I had no clue what I was doing. I wore a red and black plaid schoolgirl skirt, white knee-highs and a tight white top. Thinking about it now I basically dressed myself like a porn star, even though I didn't know it at the time. That is just what I thought looked good or maybe I just had zero fashion sense even though I was attending school for fashion. Go figure. Coming from a girl who wore pajamas to school most of the time anyway, I thought I was really dressed up for the occasion! I just wanted to look really sexy and show off what I could in the small amount of time I might have in front of the agents. In my mind, I was dressing sexy to get what I want, which was my thought process at 18 and all I really knew at the time.

I drove over to the modeling agency, which wasn't too far from my apartment in the valley. As I walked towards the agency building, I was nervous and excited at the same time. When I first walked in, it looked a bit run down and I was hoping I was in the wrong place. There were many different offices and companies along a long hallway, so it was a bit confusing as I proceeded further down the hall. I didn't see or hear anyone until I noticed one large office with a lot of desks. I hesitantly walked inside. It wasn't what I had imagined a modeling agency would be like, but I was too excited to think that it was sketchy or that someone may try to murder me. I so badly wanted it to be a modeling agency trying to sign me. Looking around the office, I noticed the walls were covered in pictures of really hot girls. I remember the whole place looking and feeling cheap, but I had never been in any type of modeling agency before so I really didn't know what to expect.

I made my way towards the main large office and as I walked down the hallway, I heard a man scream from one of the side offices in a strong New York accent, "I'll take her!" I was the only one in the hallway so I thought, "He wants to take me where?!" I was almost to the main office when a casually dressed man in his mid-thirties approached me from one of the offices. This was the same guy who yelled he wanted me. I didn't know it then, but he was an agent with the company, and walked me down to the main office as he knew I was lost. As I walked into the office, he shouted to the man sitting behind the desk, "Is she new? I want her!" At this point, I was really confused. The man behind the desk seemed like the boss in the office so I asked him if I was in the right place. I explained that I was given a business card by a man a couple days ago and that I had a meeting scheduled today. I didn't see the man from the club anywhere. The man behind the desk told me in a Southern accent that I was in the right place. He introduced himself, and asked me to sit down.

He explained that he worked with the man from the club, but that the man was a talent scout so he never really came into the office. The man behind the desk was the owner of the agency. He was a tall, thin, older gentleman with grey hair. He made me feel comfortable right away. He wasn't creepy or perverted in any way, but was very professional. He almost came across as a father figure to me. My nervousness went away, and I actually had a feeling as though I had known him for years. He asked me, "What can we do for you?" I simply told him that I was interested in modeling and I was hoping that he could help find me some modeling work. He began to explain that his agency mostly does movies. With a nervous, awkward laugh I replied, "Oh cool, that sounds fun too." He then proceeded to explain that the movies were adult movies and that he represented the performers as their agent. I innocently asked, "What do you mean?" I could barely finish my question, when I heard that strong New York accent yell from down the hall, "We book girls for porn." My heart sank.

How could I be so stupid? I was so excited to possibly be signing with a legitimate modeling agency and I began to think it was foolish of me to believe I could have a real modeling agency want to sign me. I tried to hold in my sinking feelings and very nicely explained that I was in the wrong place and that I was sorry for wasting their time. As I got up to leave, the man calmly told me how much money I could get paid per movie and I quickly sat back down. He definitely got my attention with the numbers. It was a lot of money. I was hesitant and intrigued at the same time. I was already in the office and spent the time to get ready and drive over to this meeting, so I decided it wouldn't hurt to at least get more information on it. Besides, the more I thought about it, the more I became convinced that this could actually be fun. For the next three hours, I sat in that chair being persuaded by the owner and two other agents that I should do porn, how well I would do in the industry, and how much money they could make me if I signed with them. I didn't even know they had agencies and agents for porn stars. I had dressed the part and fit the role they were looking for, I just didn't know it. I had always been money-motivated so the money they were talking about as an 18 year old seemed insane. This was a lot of money to anyone at any age, period. How much money were we talking about? About $30,000 per month or more. That's $360,000 per year!

The agents weren't scummy or pushy towards me to sign with them like some people might think (at least not in my experience). They told me to give it some thought and explained that the movies and videos would be out there forever. They even told me that if I did decide to do porn that I should tell my family because they would find out one way or another, and better that it comes from me than someone else. To me, this advice made it seem like they actually cared about me. It made me develop some trust in them and gave me a sense of belonging, which I never really felt before. At the time, I really wasn't thinking about the porn or sex part of it. I was just fixated on the amount of money I could make. In those 3 hours, I made a decision that would change my life FOREVER: I signed with a porn agency and sold my soul that same day.

The thought of making anything close to $30,000 per month was incredible to me. People might be wondering what I was thinking, but I was young, and I thought about all the cool things I could buy and do with all that money. I knew how to have fun, and I definitely knew how to get myself into things that I wasn't supposed to. I wasn't the smartest girl at 18, but when given the opportunity to make that kind of money at such a young age, it was hard to say no. At least for me it was. When we're young, we can be very impulsive and many things influence us very quickly depending on what's important to us at that time in our lives. Everyone has driving motivations. Mine was money; it's as simple as that. I didn't have my parents pay for my college or my rent, I had to depend on myself and no one else. Money isn't everything, but at that age, at that time in my life, it certainly was, or at least very close to, the top of my priorities. I was already a stripper, and if you've read my first book, *The Story of Channon Rose – Lessons Between the Lines,* you would already know that I don't have an innocent past anyway. I got enjoyment out of doing things I wasn't supposed to and I liked being different and pushing my limits. It's not like I was a virgin and jumping into this. I already had sex with people for money. This was the same thing except someone would film it. I was already dancing naked every night. Why not do a little combining and make a shitload of money? It seemed silly not to take this opportunity.

So, as it went, I made a deal with the Devil and signed my life away that day. After I signed the contract, my new agent said I needed to pick a stage name. They explained that once I started shooting movies, I could get stalkers and weirdos who would try to find me. I didn't really have time to think about a name nor did I think I needed to pick one right then and there but I had to pick a name on the spot. I needed a name that people would grow to know me as and call me for years to come (possibly the rest of my life). I knew right away that I wanted a boy's name since I like to be different, so I picked Randi, but I wanted to spell it differently so I went with an "I" instead of a "Y." My agent came up with the last name Wright, making my new stage name Randi Wright. I ended up spending most of the day in the office with the agents. They explained a lot more in depth about the industry, safety measures, and how things worked. They were very protective of me and wanted me armed with as much knowledge about the industry as possible before I began working. Never once did I ask myself, "What the hell did I get myself into?" What did come to mind though was that this was going to be awesome.

While in the office, I was also given an address where I would be getting my blood drawn and urine tested quite frequently. In order to be able to do porn, you have to get your blood and urine tested once a month for the safety of all the performers. I believe that policy has changed to every two weeks now, but I'm not exactly sure. I was definitely on the fast track to working. That same day one of the agents drove me to a medical facility called AIM (Adult Industry Medical). It was a medical office specifically for people in the adult entertainment industry. I never even knew these types of places existed. This was a whole new world and was much larger than I imagined. There's a lot more to porn than people think. You don't just show up to set and have sex while someone films it. The adult entertainment industry is a big deal, worth a lot more money than I ever imagined and things are taken a lot more seriously than you would think. I'll admit the drive over to AIM made me nervous. The thought of getting tested was scary. I hadn't always been safe when I was younger when it came to having sex, and I had unprotected sex with past boyfriends. Some of them had cheated on me, which worried me more because I had never been tested for STD's (sexually transmitted diseases) before. My mind started to overload with doubt and questions about my past and the history of my former partners. I started freaking out a little bit thinking I may have herpes or even worse, HIV or AIDS.

When we finally arrived at AIM, my agent helped me out and showed me the ropes. He brought over some paperwork for me to fill out and explained that I would pee in a cup and they would draw my blood each month at this facility. He also explained how the adult entertainment industry is my job now and that I need to be very careful with whom I choose to have sex with (outside of the industry) and that I need to always practice safe sex outside of work. He also said I need to bring a copy of my most current tests to set each time with a picture ID so that I would be able to work and they could verify that my test was clean and up to date. When you arrive on set, all the performers tests are reviewed and checked before anyone can film a scene. The tests of course need to be negative to be able to work. My sexual health was now a part of my job. Being sexually safe and smart was mandatory.

In addition to bringing your test results to set, AIM also kept all the records in their computer system. That allowed them to have access to inform anyone and everyone immediately if or when there might be any kind of problem or positive test from any of the performers. The more I learned about this profession, the more I realized how professional it was. Not only that, but everyone was really nice and down to earth. In fact, some of the coolest, most nonjudgmental people I've ever met were all from the adult entertainment industry. By this point, my entire experience in this new industry wasn't bad at all. After I filled out all of my paperwork I was called back into one of the medical offices. I was given a cup to pee in, went to the restroom, peed in the cup and went into a little room. I was sweating and getting even more nervous at this point. All I could think about over and over in my head was, "Please don't have HIV, please don't have herpes." I'm surprised I didn't pass out right then and there before they even drew my blood! As the phlebotomist withdrew my blood, I kept thinking, "Okay, if I have an STD, which of my ex's should I kill first?" Fortunately, the blood draw didn't hurt and it went by pretty quickly. My agent paid the $120 for the cost of the tests and we were on our merry way. An interesting aspect of testing at AIM is that you get the results the next day, which is much faster than if you were to test anywhere else.

On the drive back to the agency, my agent told me he wanted to introduce me to some porn companies the next day. These visits were also known as "Go-see's." My agent was hustling for sure and they were making things happen fast. Once we got back to the office, the agency needed to take some nude photos for their website. I knocked out some nude pictures for them and we were done for the day. Within a few hours, I signed with a porn agency, created a stage name, got tested for STD's, took nude photos for agency representation, and set up porn company meetings for the very next day. Life was moving very fast and I loved every minute of it.

Lessons I've learned:

- Practice SAFE sex from the moment you lose your virginity. We all think that the person we are dating, or are in love with is clean but you really never know unless you see an up-to-date negative STD test, so use protection.
- If you plan to have unprotected sex make the person you are with get tested for STD's first and make them show you that their test is negative. Also, if you don't plan to get pregnant make sure you are on some form of birth control. You don't have to do porn to get tested often and be able to prove you are in good health to the person you are being intimate with. Take it from me, it is an AWFUL feeling not knowing if you have an STD. It might feel awkward to ask someone to be tested before you hook up with them, but I can promise you it is more awkward to have or get an STD that you are stuck with for the rest of your life.
- Don't date anyone that treats you less than the prince or princess you are. A lot of times, we can feel insecure for whatever reason and we think we aren't good enough, or pretty enough, or skinny enough, or whatever the case may be and we tell ourselves that

we don't deserve someone amazing to date. I am here to tell you that YOU ARE ENOUGH and you DO deserve someone awesome who treats you like royalty, so don't settle for anything less. I made that mistake and it cost me years of unhappiness and I wish someone would have told me what I just told you.

CHAPTER 2

My 1st Day as a Porn Star

"All things in life are difficult before they are easy."

-Thomas Fuller

The next day I drove back to my agent's office so we could get the day started and meet with the different porn companies that he had previously set up times with. I had a million thoughts in my head on my drive over to meet with him. What if the people that worked at these porn companies think I'm ugly? Is my outfit slutty enough? What if I freeze up or have an anxiety attack while I'm in one of my meetings? They might think I'm a total freak! I didn't know how I was supposed to act. I kept thinking to myself am I supposed to act like myself? Should I put on a "porn" persona? Maybe I should act like a slutty airhead? I didn't know what they expected from me or how to act so it made me really nervous. I was used to thinking of myself in a very negative way. You can say I was a pro at self-sabotage. I didn't have very good self-esteem about my looks or myself in general. I would talk down to myself. I think it was a protective mechanism I had for myself in hopes that I would not be as disappointed if I were to be rejected by one of these porn companies. It really wasn't a healthy way to view myself or live my life. I think a lot of people go through those same feelings at some point in their life though. Either way, in this case I didn't want to get my hopes up too high just to be on the safe side.

I finally pulled up to my agent's office, hopped into my agent's car and we headed to the first porn company he had scheduled. My very first go-see was Wicked Pictures. Once again, I started getting nervous and doubting myself and I think my agent could sense that I was anxious. He said not to worry and that they were going to absolutely love me, and as soon as they saw me they would want to book me a lot of work. What he said calmed my nerves and gave me the confidence boost that I so desperately needed. After spending so much time with him yesterday I knew that he was pretty experienced in the industry, so if he said something, I took what he said seriously. A short drive later, we pulled into the parking lot at the Wicked Pictures office. Their office was also in the valley. The San Fernando Valley was also known as "Porn Capital of The World" or "Porn Valley." There was a time when almost all porn was made in the valley. The valley just so happens to be where I was born and raised. What a shocker, right?! It's like I was meant to do porn!

We parked the car and got out, and as I was walking up to their office, I realized that people would never know this was a porn company. It looked like your average industrial office building. It didn't have the porn company's name on the outside so you would never know that the office housed a billion-dollar porn company. As we were getting ready to walk into Wicked's office, my agent turned to look at me and said, "How does it feel, your first day as a porn star?" I just laughed at him because I definitely didn't feel like a porn star. I felt like such a newbie and there was still so much that I had to learn about this industry. I was just getting started. I always thought the label "porn star" was funny anyway, because the title itself claimed you as a "star" no matter what. In mainstream Hollywood, a "star" is a big time, A-list actor or actress. In porn, everyone's already a star even if your acting sucks.

My agent and I were now at the front door and we headed inside the office. As we walked in, I looked around the office and I was shocked as it looked totally different on the inside than it did on the outside. It was REALLY nice inside. It showed me a little taste of how much money was actually in porn. We soon met with the owner of Wicked Pictures in his office. I wasn't expecting to meet with one of the owners. I just assumed I would be meeting with someone who worked there. When I walked into his office, I was blown away at some of the sports and movie memorabilia he had. There was a life-sized medieval armor statue. It was like a museum in this guy's office. The owner wasn't super friendly towards me and he seemed like he was busy, so he didn't make too much small talk. He quickly asked me to get naked, which I did without hesitation, and then he asked me to spin around so he could see what I looked like. He said I had a nice body and then he handed me a script. That was when I freaked out. I didn't care about taking my clothes off, but I wasn't prepared to read lines. He assured me that he just wanted to hear me read the first few lines with him. I was more nervous about reading lines than I was about getting naked in front of the owner of this huge porn company!

I read the lines in my shaky nervous voice and of course did a terrible job. That was no surprise. I was no actress. He thanked me for coming in and I left thinking he hated me. He wasn't as friendly as my agents were to me. He was colder and more distant, and didn't seem like he had a lot of time to be meeting with me. I definitely didn't feel good about my first go-see. Fortunately, it didn't matter too much because my agent had us scheduled for multiple visits that day. We went to several other porn companies and the meetings were all pretty similar. I would walk in, shake their hand, introduce myself, get naked for them, do a little spin and then leave. It was kind of weird, but fun at the same time. I loved the attention and all the people telling me how great I looked. My ego was rocketed into high gear after so many people said I looked sexy naked. It was a huge confidence booster for me. I never felt proud of my body because we are all our own worst critics, but that day made me feel even better about getting into porn. After all, these people saw naked girls on a daily basis so to hear that was awesome. It was a cool first day as a "porn star," but it wasn't over yet.

Later that day, after we were all done with our meetings, I was back in my car heading home when I got a call from the owner of my agency. I answered my phone and he said in his Southern accent, "Darling, you are likely going to be booked solid with work for the next 30 days." I was shocked, nervous, and excited all at the same time! He said he hadn't stopped getting calls to book me. Between the go-see's, my pictures posted on the agency website, and the e-mails that were sent out introducing me as new talent, he was flooded with calls. I was about to be rich! That's all I could think about. I also felt so loved as weird as that sounds. I felt like I was wanted since people were requesting me specifically. I instantly felt like I finally found a place that I belonged, and felt wanted and needed. All of which made me very happy because growing up I never felt like I belonged anywhere. I never felt special. I felt like an outcast.

This came out the first month I started doing porn. I was on the cover of L.A. X...PRESS!

The owner then told me that two companies were fighting over who could shoot my first movie. Since I was in such high demand, I was able to charge extra for my first scene, which would take place the very next day! He also told me that he received my STD results and they had come back clean, which was a huge relief. It meant I didn't have to kill any ex-boyfriends, but it also confirmed that I was ready to shoot my very first porn movie. Or was I?

The thought of shooting my first porn movie terrified me. As excited as I was about the money, it was overshadowed by my anxiety about the shoot. That evening, my agent sent me my info (call sheet) for the shoot the very next day. My call time (time to be on the movie set) was 8 a.m. I was also informed that hair and makeup was on set, which means they have a team of people to do my hair and makeup and pick out my clothes. I was told to bring some different outfits, lingerie, and heels. I was shooting the box cover and doing a boy-girl scene for the porn company Red Light District. A boy-girl scene is basically exactly how it sounds, one guy and one girl. I was also booked for a second scene that would be later in the afternoon that same day for the same company. Usually, when you shoot porn, a female performer will do one scene per day for a movie. They use several different performers to make several separate scenes. Those several scenes make up one whole movie. I was then given the set location and the name of who I would be working with, although I had no idea who they were anyway because I was brand new and hadn't watched enough porn before to know who it was. I hadn't met any other talent (performers) yet. My agent also told me I would be making $3,350 for one day of shooting. That was a lot of money to me. Especially for only one day! I spent the rest of the evening getting ready for the next day but I was so anxious that I could barely sleep that night.

The next morning I woke up super early and so incredibly nervous. I could barely breathe I was so anxious. There was no way in hell I was going to be able to do this sober. I was too nervous to eat so instead of having breakfast, I decided to go buy a bottle of Smirnoff Vodka on my way to set. Classy, I know. I arrived extra early so I could drink beforehand in my car on an empty stomach. I may have been drunk on my first day, but at least I was on time. I functioned pretty well because I was drinking daily when I danced at the club. I pulled into the parking lot of the set location around 6 a.m. Sitting in the driver's seat, I chugged straight out of the bottle. The alcohol definitely helped me out. By the time I was buzzed, I felt ready to walk onto my first porn set. I was so self-conscious walking into a building with no makeup on, especially when I was being paid to look sexy. I didn't know what to expect or how I would perform but I knew once that liquid courage fully hit me, I would be good to go. When I got drunk I became confident, had more fun, felt sexier and willing to do things I would never do sober...like shoot a porn scene!

When I first walked in, I met the photographer, videographer, makeup artist, and a personal assistant who made a copy of my test and my ID. I filled out a model release form, liability paperwork, and a couple other forms. I then had to go over outfits and what I was going to wear for my "pretty girl" pictures. These are the pictures that you take before the scene that are used for the box cover, website, magazines, and any promo. Once we had the outfit picked out for the pictures, we then picked out an outfit to be used in the actual video. As soon as that was all done, it was time for hair and makeup. What girl doesn't love sitting in a chair while you get your hair and makeup professionally done, right? We next shot the pretty girl pictures. I enjoyed shooting the pictures, and it helped me feel a little more comfortable being on set for the first time. Not to mention it's fun to have your hair and makeup done and have your pictures taken. There were lights, camera, and a photographer; it was a full modeling shoot, or at least it was for me. It went pretty quickly, but all of it was enjoyable.

The whole time I tried to pretend I wasn't drunk. I didn't know if they could tell or not, but honestly I was too drunk to care. Another few hours went by and it was finally time to shoot my scene. One thing I learned that first day was that sometimes you could be on set for a very long time before you actually shoot your scene. You might be waiting around for hours. It was awhile before we started shooting and I started to feel sick from drinking cheap vodka on an empty stomach since 6 a.m., so I went outside and walked over to the side of the building and threw up. Then I just walked back to the shoot like nothing happened. I did that twice that day, but kept on drinking. A few minutes before my scene, I met the guy that I was shooting with. He was good-looking, super nice, and respectful. I was still pretty nervous even with all the Smirnoff in me. I pulled it together and walked onto the set of my first porn movie. Once we started shooting, it really wasn't bad at all. It was actually pretty fun. He was very experienced, and even though I wasn't, the alcohol kicked in and I did what I thought I was supposed to do. It wasn't bad at all and before I knew it, we were done. I had just shot my very first porn scene!

My workday wasn't over though. I still had another scene to shoot later that afternoon. I took a shower on set, and the makeup artist touched up my hair and makeup. We picked out new outfits, and went through the same getting ready process as we did earlier in the morning. I was shooting another boy-girl scene, which meant new male talent. I didn't know it at the time, but the male actor in the next scene was known for sending girls to the hospital because he was so rough during scenes! I'm glad they didn't tell me that because I would have definitely chickened out, especially since I was new. I soon met Erik Everhard, the actor I was shooting with, and was ready to rock my next scene. We walked onto set and started our scene.

At this point I was pretty hammered, since I had been drinking all day, and I was tired from waking up so early. Plus, shooting even one scene a day takes a lot out of you. Something very different happened during this scene though. This second scene was nothing like my first. I don't know what got into me, but it was like another person was in my body. Who was this person? Have we met before?! All I know is that I owned that set. If people didn't know any better, they would have thought I was a seasoned veteran. I took over that scene. I was crazy, but in a good way, a way that shows up really well on camera for a porn scene. I was so crazy that I made Erik Everhard tap out! The porn stud who is known for being rough called a timeout during our scene because he couldn't keep up with me! The scene went amazing. Red Light District was overly impressed with my performance and immediately people on set were saying that I was the next big thing in porn. It was absolutely mind-blowing.

This was my very first movie and I was on the box cover

The next day, I was sore all over. When I say sore, I mean my whole body and my cupcake (aka my vagina) were super sore. However, I had made over $3,000 in one day, so it was totally worth it to me. I got a call from my agent saying that Red Light loved me and not only did they already book me again, but they were so impressed with my scene that they wanted to put it into the Paris Hilton sex tape. Being in the Paris video would skyrocket my porn career overnight.

Here's the lowdown on celebrity sex tapes. When a celebrity needs publicity, or money or whatever, the celebrity will film a sex scene, amateur-style. Once the video is shot, the celebrity will then sign the rights over to a porn company (whoever will pay the most usually). This could be for hundreds of thousands of dollars, or even into the million-dollar range, depending on the celebrity. From there, a big publicity stunt is created to say there is "leaked" sex footage. It naturally draws in a huge demand of people who want to see the footage. You get the idea.

To my knowledge, what happened with the Paris Hilton sex tape was that Red Light purchased the rights to the Paris footage. Well, it just so happened that this purchase occurred around the time when I shot my first scenes with Red Light. They loved my scene so much that they wanted to add it into the Paris tape as bonus footage. The DVD was called "1 Night in Paris". As soon as that DVD was released, it was everywhere. It was a huge deal and I got quite popular very quickly from it. People knew the name Randi Wright immediately and I had barely started in the business. I worked almost every day for a month straight. I should add I quickly decided I would drop out of college. I was going to FIDM, a fashion design school in LA. When I was graduating high school, I thought it would be fun to be a fashion designer but I quickly learned that school was taking up a lot of my time. It was also expensive. I figured that I liked this new job way more, was making more money this way, and was over school. I felt that I'm only young once, and that I can go to school at any age.

In my new life, I was making SO much money. I'll admit that I really enjoyed doing porn. I didn't love the early call times, but the lifestyle was awesome. I was living like a movie star in Hollywood, but without the hassle of being a "celebrity." I didn't have to worry about being stopped and asked for pictures, and I didn't have to worry about paparazzi. Not only was I living this awesome lifestyle, but I was also meeting celebrities and partying with important people. I was doing photoshoots everyday, I was on camera daily, and regularly doing interviews. I was seeing myself on DVD covers and on the cover of magazines. It was all happening so fast. I didn't have to worry about paying bills or if I would have enough money for rent. I could buy whatever I wanted. I stopped looking at the price tag on things when I went shopping. I was even able to purchase a brand new Ford F150 truck and have it custom painted hot pink.

My hot pink truck before I had it lifted

I got it lifted and put some sick new rims and tires on it. It stood out everywhere, and made a few cameos in my porn videos! My truck quickly became well known and everyone in the valley and Hollywood knew it belonged to a porn star. So much for privacy. I had always wanted a hot pink truck and at the time I was 18 years old, so you know, it was totally appropriate! No one else had a pink truck back then so I thought it was pretty cool.

I was learning very quickly about the porn business and started making good friends in the industry. Everything was going great. I was having a lot of fun until I got a phone call that would stop my wild life dead in its tracks.

Lessons I've learned:

- Try something new even if it scares you. You may surprise yourself and be really good at it.

- Don't drink straight vodka on an empty stomach unless you want to get sick.

- People in sex work, or adult film, whatever you want to call it, aren't all bad people or all on drugs. In fact, some of them are the coolest, nicest, most down-to-earth people you will ever meet. I have met people from all walks of life and these people were some of the friendliest and least judgmental I've ever known.

CHAPTER 3

I Love You. Just Kidding. I Hate You.

"When someone shows you who they are, believe them the first time."

\- Maya Angelou

My phone rang and as I looked down to see who it was, I immediately knew the number. It wasn't a stranger, or an unknown number calling me. It was someone I knew well, very well actually. But why the call and why now? My heart raced as I quickly went back and forth in my head on whether I should answer the phone or not. That familiar number calling was my ex-boyfriend Joe. I think most of us know that feeling when about a dozen questions come into your mind within seconds as to why they might be calling. I think I was scared that he found out I was doing porn and that he would make me feel bad about it. Even though I was happy and we were broken up, he was someone I cared about and if he were to tell me negative things, it would still probably affect me in some way. Even with all my anxiety and worry about why he was calling me, my curiosity took over and I still wanted to know what he had to say. I caved in and answered the phone.

"Hello?" I said. "Hey, what's up?" he replied.

Just the sound of his voice made my heart pound. It felt as though it was going to pound right out of my chest. I was afraid he could feel it and hear it through the phone. I had so many emotions happening and I was just trying to stay as calm as I could at the moment, after all I still didn't know where this conversation might lead. I don't think up until this point I had given it much thought, but once on the phone and hearing his voice it became clear to me that I was still very much in love with him. I actually hated the fact that it was true, and I hated myself for still loving him, but it was what it was, and there wasn't much I could do about it. You can't always help who you love, fall in love with, or stay in love with even when you know they aren't good for you. Even though I was technically an adult, I was still learning about love and emotions.

He was bad for me and I knew it, but he had a way of drawing me towards him and getting me to do things for him. I was anxiously waiting for him to tell me what he wanted. I wasn't expecting or really prepared for what he was about to bring up. He asked what I've been up to and I simply said, "Keeping busy." He replied, "So, I heard you're doing porn now." My heart stopped. I didn't really know what to say and didn't really want to get into details, so I simply replied, "Yup." He asked how it was and I told him the truth, that it was cool and that I was making a lot of money. He said, "Sweet, you down to hang out later?" I was a bit shocked by his reply and that he even wanted to hang out after I just told him I was doing porn. I really expected to get torn to pieces with him calling me names or the typical "You're better than that," but those words never came out of his mouth. He simply wanted to see me. The fact that he was chill about everything and didn't try and make me feel bad was pretty cool. We ended up meeting up that day.

Joe and I

Seeing him brought back even more feelings and I think that he felt the same way. Three days later, we were back together again. Getting back together wasn't that simple though. A lot had changed in the short amount of time that we were apart, and not just on my end. If we were going to make this work I would have to make dramatic, life-altering decisions and sacrifice a lot. Much more than he would need to sacrifice. While we were broken up, Joe had moved four hours away to his parents' lake house near Lake Nacimiento in California. He wanted me to move up there with him and quit doing porn. Well, it's crazy what people will do for love. The power he had over me was still very strong and as you might guess, I was willing to do it for him. I called my agent and told him I was quitting porn and that I was moving away. He was very sad to see me go, but wanted me to know that if I ever wanted to come back that I would have a job in porn waiting for me.

My plan was to move up north to be with Joe and go back to school. I wanted to do something different this time around, so I decided that I wanted to attend beauty school, as it had always been an interest of mine. I also needed to find an apartment, as I wouldn't be able to move into Joe's parents' house with him. Joe's parents were really religious so they wouldn't allow that. The closest real town was Paso Robles. Paso Robles is about halfway between Los Angeles and San Francisco. It's sort of in the country, as there are a lot of wineries, farms, and open land. It's a very small town, and most of the people who live there all know each other and know everyone's business. It felt like the middle of NOWHERE for a city girl like me, which is probably not the best place for a girl who has done porn to try and start over.

I had no idea what I was getting myself into but I didn't care. I was in love and willing to go to great lengths to be with Joe. I broke my lease on my current apartment in the valley, which cost me thousands of dollars, and signed a new lease on a new apartment in Paso Robles and enrolled in beauty school as I had planned. I packed up all my stuff in my hot pink lifted truck, moved out of my old place and drove up to Paso Robles. I left everything behind to be with him: my family, friends, a job, and a lifestyle I really loved. It turned out that my lifestyle was pretty cool in LA, but not so much in Paso Robles. I stuck out like a sore thumb and within the first week everyone knew who I was and that I had done porn. Whenever I drove in town and had my windows down, the residents would yell obscenities at me. Sometimes women would yell out the titles of some of my porn movies or just yell, "PORN STAR!" Or "SLUT!" I did my best to ignore it and not let it get to me. I would just shake my head and think to myself that her husband probably jerks off to me.

I was trying to begin a new life for myself, but it was drastically different than what I had been doing for the past few months. I was out of porn, back in school, in a new area, and had just gotten back together with an old boyfriend. I was trying to settle down from where I had been in my life, but I felt like the people in Paso Robles just saw me as a porn star. It was annoying, but I tried to focus on school, where the only thing I learned was that I still hated school. I soon found out in beauty school that I hated doing hair. I absolutely hated it. It definitely was not for me. I decided to switch into their esthetician program after a few months in regular beauty school because I wanted to do makeup and the school counselor suggested I do an esthetician program, since their small town didn't have a makeup school. I then found out after being in esthetician school for a while that I wasn't into skin care either. I lost focus easily and was unhappy, so I just did everyone's makeup during class. I was trying to find my new path, but was struggling. I wanted to like being normal, but I just felt like I didn't fit in and I didn't feel happy in beauty school. Things between Joe and I were going really well, but my education wasn't. I think Joe was happy with the fact that I was enrolled in school and not doing porn anymore and that I had moved closer to be with him. So while one aspect of my life was great, the other not so much, but I was in love with him and that was enough for me at the time.

Life in Paso Robles definitely moved at a slower pace than LA, which also took some getting used to. My life had never been boring up until living in Paso Robles. I figured that my so-called "boring life" wouldn't last long as something crazy was always bound to happen to me. Any time my life was getting boring something crazy would happen and I was right. This time I had missed my period. All kinds of thoughts raced through my head but the main thought was if I was pregnant. I immediately rushed my ass to the nearest grocery store and bought a pregnancy test. I then raced home and peed on that stick as fast as I could and waited. Then waited some more. If you've ever taken a pregnancy test, those minutes feel like FOREVER. Slowly the lines on the stick started to show. There was one dark line and one faint line. Did this mean I was pregnant? Were they supposed to be the same darkness? I didn't know so I called the 1-800 help line number on the box to find out. I had never been pregnant before so I had no idea how the pregnancy tests worked. Finally, the lady came on the line and said if there is a second line, even if it's faint, it is considered positive. OMG, it was positive! Holy shit, I'm pregnant. Did I just say that? Did this just happen? I'm 19 and pregnant! I was actually really excited. I was so excited that I called Joe immediately and told him we needed to talk. As I waited for him to come over, it again felt like it took forever. I was so excited to tell him the news! When he got in the door I could barely contain my excitement. I told him as soon as he walked in and I showed him the pee stick to show him that I was serious and not pranking him. He didn't believe me so he made me take another test in front of him, which irritated me. When the results came up positive, Joe was shocked and surprised, but not in the way I had hoped. He wasn't excited, he wasn't hopeful, in fact he wasn't happy at all. He told me I needed to have an abortion. There really wasn't much else he said after that. I was in such shock that I couldn't say a word. I was holding my tears back.

The truth was, I was devastated. My heart sank in my chest and it felt like the whole world was crashing down on me. I wasn't expecting that response from him. I knew we weren't married, but we were in love and I thought it would be a happy surprise. I was naive and learning things the hard way as usual. It's hard to explain the feeling I had. To have so much joy and excitement, about something so big, and to not have the feeling reciprocated from someone you love is an awful, terrible feeling. I was devastated by not only his reaction, but that he wanted to kill our baby. This was something that we had created, something that was part of us. I still didn't know what to say to him. This whole pregnancy was quickly turning into a nightmare. I knew he didn't want me to keep our baby, but I thought maybe if I give him a week to think about it, he might change his mind.

A week went by and I couldn't be more wrong. Things had just gotten worse. From the moment I told Joe that I was pregnant he turned into a monster. He didn't allow me over at his parents' lake house because if they found out they would make us keep the baby and get married. He wouldn't let me talk to any of his friends. He didn't want anyone to know that I was pregnant. I had no one to talk to and I needed someone to comfort me from all these terrible emotions. I moved my whole life to the middle of nowhere to be with the love of my life and now that I am pregnant he wanted nothing to do with me. Clearly, we didn't feel the same way about each other or want the same things from our relationship. I decided that it was time to call my mom.

I called my mom and explained what was happening. My mom wasn't happy about me being pregnant either and at that point I gave up hope for the baby growing inside me. My mom convinced me that I was too young and not ready to have a baby. She told me that I needed to finish school and have a solid relationship or career before I brought a baby into this world. She made valid points, but something inside me made it very hard for me to think about killing my own baby, especially a baby with someone that I loved. It was all really hard for me to deal with. I felt that I was grown up and ready for a baby, but looking back, I was still very young. I had two of the closest, most important people to me telling me the same thing, that I needed to have an abortion and that I shouldn't keep this baby. Did they know something I didn't? Was I missing something here? Had I not thought this through as they possibly had? I questioned everything at this point. I thought I could have this baby and make it work, but my mom and Joe strongly disagreed with me. I was alone.

One thing I knew for sure was that if Joe really made me go through with having an abortion, I would be done with him for good. There would be no way I could love him after that. I was heartbroken by the entire situation. I was hurting so badly inside emotionally, and I knew that I would continue to hurt either way. No matter what choice I made, I was losing something. I had to make a decision though. I decided to move back to LA. I just couldn't handle the small town and with everything going on, I had to leave. Once again, I broke my lease on my apartment in Paso Robles and found a new apartment in LA. In addition to that, I dropped out of beauty school, which wasn't hard since I hated it anyway. I got settled into my new place back in LA and was at least closer to my mom and family for the next big decision I had to make. I finally decided to go through with the abortion. It was one of the hardest decisions I'd made at that point of my life. My mom set up an appointment for me to have the abortion privately and she even offered to pay for it. Joe knew I was going through with it, and didn't even have the decency to be there with me on the day of my surgery. He didn't even offer to help cover the costs. What a piece of shit. I cried the entire night before my surgery and the entire morning of my surgery, and was still crying even when I woke up from my procedure after the anesthesia wore off. After the abortion, we stopped talking. I later found out that he was cheating on me the entire time I was living in Paso Robles. I fucking hated him for that, but mainly because of the abortion. His encouraging me to get an abortion made me lose my love for him. At the time, there wasn't even a small piece of my heart left that had feelings for that man, and after all he did to me and put me through it makes sense why. Fuck you Joe. I mean, um, I wish you nothing but the very best.

Lessons I've learned:

- Sometimes you will make decisions in life that you regret and you will have to live with those choices you make forever.

- Being in a toxic relationship can feel like you are being mentally broken over and over again but instead of feeling defeated I have chosen to see the positive aspects of being in that type of relationship. Joe taught me to be resilient and has taught me the ability now to bounce back from adversity or difficult events in my life.

- I now always try to see the good in the bad things that happen to us or try to turn a negative situation into something positive. It takes practice but over time you get better at it. You should start to try and incorporate that into your life.

CHAPTER 4

After the Abortion

"Fear is temporary. Regret is forever."

- Unknown

I felt broken, and it was because I truly was. That asshole had hurt me so badly in the past, but this was a whole new level of pain and hurt I was going through. I felt as though a piece of me died the day I had that abortion and to this day, it still hurts. I don't hurt because of Joe, but because of what was taken from me… a child, a son or a daughter, who could have been about 13 years old today. I remained very close with my mom during this time and I talked to her a lot. My mom made me feel like I did the right thing. Some days I would cry nonstop to her and she would keep telling me over and over all the reasons why I made the right choice. I felt like I did the right thing in my head, but in my heart it felt differently. I felt so much sadness. It's really hard to explain the feeling and put it into words, but it's something I will always have to live with. Your head and your heart are both so strong and influential in your life, yet they don't always agree. I guess throughout our lives we just try and listen to whichever one is the strongest at that moment, and hope that they make the right decisions for us.

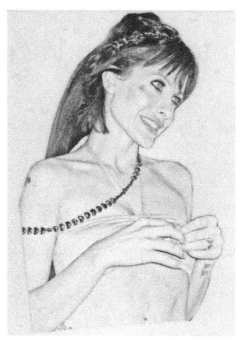

Once upon a time she smiled in pain

"We all make mistakes, have struggles, and even regret things in our past. But you are not your mistakes, you are not your struggles, and you are here NOW with the power to shape your day and your future."

- Steve Maraboli

As the weeks went by, I started to run low on money because LA isn't a cheap place to live, and I hadn't been working. Not only that, but between breaking my lease, a deposit on another new apartment and general living expenses, it all added up quickly. I decided to get back into the life I had before I left and to start doing porn again. I needed to work, I needed to get my mind on other things, and I missed it. I had a lot of fun, made great money, and actually had a good life before I left for Paso Robles, so why not get back into it. My agent had also kept the door open for me to come back and was really kind when I left, so I felt comfortable calling him to ask for my old job back. I called my agent and he was so happy to hear from me. He said he could get me back to work that same week! Before I knew it I was back to work and on set almost every day again, racking in tons of money. It was like I had never left. Keeping busy and working a lot really helped me during that time of my life. I also felt more in control of my life again, because whatever I was doing was for me, and nobody else. I wasn't worried about a boyfriend, or anyone else for that matter.

Once I started working again, I got so used to having my hair and makeup done on set that I practically forgot how to do my own hair and makeup when I wasn't working. It got to a point when I just started paying my favorite hair and makeup artist from set to do my hair and makeup when I went out in my personal life for events or to go clubbing or whatever. Did that get to be expensive? Yep, but my spending didn't stop there. I was making a lot of money, but I was also good at spending it. I was going through my money almost as fast as it was coming in. It was so easy and fast to make money that if I spent it, I felt I could just make it back again quickly anyway. I went from being a broke college student to living quite the lavish lifestyle. I was young and dumb and not smart with my money. At 19 years old, you don't really think about being old or saving money, or at least I wasn't.

19 year old Channon

I was buying expensive clothes, bags, and living in the nicest apartment complex in the valley. Money and materialistic things aren't everything in life, but I was feeling happy again, happier than I had been in a long time. Maybe it was from the money, maybe it was my busy schedule, or maybe it was simply that I was in high demand at work. I felt wanted and special again, and that was everything to me. That's what made me happy. It might sound crazy to most people, but it feels good to feel like you are doing something to make other people happy and feel good. Adult films do that for a lot of people.

We are trained to think of porn as this taboo thing that no one talks about, but we all know everyone watches it. We're taught from a young age to think that it's bad and looked down upon, and that's what we end up thinking without even giving it a second thought. For whatever reason, I don't see porn the way most people do. I see it as acting out something that turns on whoever is watching. Seriously, what is so wrong with that? We watch all types of movies and shows that give us a variety of feelings. Artists and actors can bring out emotions of happiness, sadness, fear, excitement, or any of our other emotions and they can do that depending on the scene or the moment. So why is porn, sex, or feelings of intimacy labeled differently? Do you think it's degrading and wrong when mainstream celebrities do a simulated sex scene? You are probably thinking the answer is no because they are just acting. Well guess what, whether you want to believe it or not, porn is acting, it's just more detailed and instead of implying that sex occurred like a mainstream movie would, the sex actually occurs. The performers are still acting out a part written out by a script, or as instructed by a director. At the end of the day, it's acting, even if it's bad acting. Sex is a part of life. Without it, you wouldn't be here and neither would I.

Since I viewed porn as a job and acting out a scene, rather than this terrible taboo thing, I actually enjoyed working at my job. I believe that's one of the main reasons I stayed in the industry a lot longer than most women do. I was in the porn industry for about 8 to 9 years. However, just because I liked doing porn doesn't mean it was always sunshine and rainbows. It definitely had its rough days and there were a lot of pros and cons that came with being a porn star.

CHAPTER 5

How My Parents Found Out I Did Porn

Despite my own relaxed personal views regarding porn and the industry, I knew that the majority of people didn't see things the same way as I did. However, I didn't know my parents' thoughts on the subject. To be honest, it's not really a conversation that most people have with their parents, but you can expect the stigma that sort of comes with porn actors and adult movies. Since I felt that it was so looked down upon, I didn't want to tell my parents because I didn't want them to be disappointed in me (again). I stopped counting the times I had disappointed my parents a long time ago. Even though I still hadn't told them, I knew I would have to at some point. I didn't want them to find out on their own before I could tell them personally and explain myself if need be. It would be pretty awkward if they found out on their own. I could only imagine one of them saying that they were watching some stuff and my vagina popped up on the screen!

I remember the day I told my mom for the first time that I was doing porn. I was driving home from work and she called me to just check in and say hi. Calling to say hi and check in with me was a regular thing she did, and she still does it to this day. I don't know why but I hated hiding things from my mom. I felt like I was lying, even though it was more like omitting information. Though in my younger years I would straight up lie to her face, keeping things from her felt weird now and I didn't like it. Maybe we had already gone through so much, or maybe I was older. I don't really know but at this point in my life I had this insatiable feeling to tell her EVERYTHING. To this day, it's the same way and she probably knows more about me and what I'm feeling than anyone else. I already knew when I picked up the phone that day that I was going to tell her I was doing porn. I remember answering the phone and I was sweating and I don't remember anything she said when I picked up. I was trying so hard to figure out how I was going to break the news to her that her first-born child was doing porn. I was stuck in my own head and my thoughts and mind were racing. How do you even break that news to someone? What do you say? Do you do it in person or over the phone? Do they need to sit down? LOL. Well, it went down over the phone like this, "So Mom umm, well, you know... umm, I'm doing porn now." That's how it came out, very elegant. I didn't plan what I was going to say obviously, but I knew I just needed to get it out there. The best part was her response. She immediately said, "I figured you were doing something like that because I was wondering where you were getting all that money from." I asked her if she was mad and she responded with, "As long as you aren't doing anything illegal and you are saving your money, then I'm fine with it." Are you kidding me!? She was so cool about it and I was not expecting that response at all. After that conversation, I felt like I could tell my mom anything and everything. From there on out that's what I did, and to this day I still do the same thing. My dad on the other hand was a different story.

I wasn't as close to my dad but I really wanted to tell him, but I just never found the right time. Keep in mind, I was getting very popular in porn so it was only a matter of time until he would find out, regardless of if I personally told him or not. Well, time moves forward quickly and he found out before I got to tell him myself. We had planned to meet up for dinner one evening, nothing out of the ordinary or special, just to say hi and catch up. I remember when I saw him he casually said in his most normal calm voice that earlier in the day he had been working on Sunset Boulevard. He said he dropped by a magazine stand to get a workout magazine and as he was looking around he saw me on the cover of one of the magazines. I guess it goes without saying that I wasn't on the cover of a bodybuilding muscle magazine. He said he picked it up but as soon as he read "Randi's wet pussy" he put two and two together and didn't open it up. Thank God! Thankfully it was one of the magazines in the plastic so you couldn't open it up anyways. So what did he do? He bought my porn magazine! He handed me the magazine that he had purchased and said, "I thought you would want it and don't worry I didn't open it, it's still in the plastic." I was dying on the inside when he handed me the magazine, but he was acting so normal about it so I did too and I simply replied, "Cool, thanks Dad." I didn't know what else to say. I knew this day would come at some point and now it finally had.

So my parent's both knew about me doing porn now, which was honestly a HUGE relief, and as odd as it was, they were both cool about it which made it easier for me to be ok with it too. As time went on, the rest of my family found out one way or another and it just became a known thing. Channon does porn. I was pretty lucky to have such a loving and accepting family. In fact I never had one person in my family tell me that what I was doing was wrong. They all continued to love me for me and not treat me any differently. Maybe they were so used to me being a fuck-up that this was not a surprise. Most likely they were probably just happy that I wasn't in jail.

CHAPTER 6

Pornfessional

By the time I was 19-20 years old I was basically a pornfessional. I had shot so many scenes in such a short period of time that it had felt as though I had been in the industry for many years. Within my first year or two, I knew almost everyone in the industry and had worked for almost every company. There weren't very many agents in the industry back then and I was still with my original agent I had started with. A bigger and better agent had approached me several times in the past but I decided to stay with my original agent until now. I slowly began to realize that my original agency wasn't the best business-wise for me, but they did get me to where I was and they had treated me very well. I had loyalty to them for that, but at the same time I felt like my time with them might be up. They felt like a second family to me and I didn't want to feel like I was betraying them. My old agent would take all of us girls out to eat now and then, and it was a comfortable environment with good people. I didn't want to hurt anyone's feelings, but business is business and I wanted to do more, work with larger companies, and continue to have new opportunities. The agent that had approached me several times in the past was at the time the best agent around. I was in the industry now for some time so I had information on a lot of companies and agents, compared to when I first signed with my first agency I didn't know anybody or anything.

The agent that had approached me had a reputation for not only representing the best girls in the industry, but also getting the best jobs for them. The new agent explained how I would do much better with him, make more money, and have more opportunities to work for bigger companies like Playboy and Hustler. After some thought and enough time to weigh my options, I did what I thought was best for my career. I decided to leave my original agent and sign with the new agency. My new agent promised a lot, and he delivered. It was quite a big change. The new agent's office was so much nicer and more professional, and the overall feel was much more business-oriented. Shortly after signing with my new agent, he got me an audition for Playboy TV! You don't normally audition for porn jobs, but this wasn't a porn job, this was to host a show on Playboy TV. It would shoot five days a week at Playboy studios and I didn't even have to have sex. Not that I didn't like sex, but it does get tiring and you get sore down there. I didn't know how I would do on the audition but I was really excited. My agent told me not to get my hopes up because there were A LOT of girls auditioning, but he thought I would be a good fit so he signed me up.

I was so nervous on the day of that audition. This was something very different for me, and I knew there would be a lot of competition. I remembered what my agent had said about not getting my hopes up so I went in to it not really expecting much. High hopes or not, I was still really nervous when I arrived to the audition. I didn't think I would get the part but I was still really happy that my agent had delivered on getting me the audition in the first place. Looking back on it now I think my doubt helped me a little because I went in with a fuck-it attitude and just had fun with it. I didn't have much (or any) information about the audition, so I couldn't really prepare for it in advance. They like to keep the upcoming shows quiet and don't tell many people about what shows they're working on. You only find out what you're auditioning for just before you go in front of them on camera for the audition. I walked in to about 30 people that I would be auditioning in front of and just before they turned the cameras on they told me it was a comedy show I was auditioning for. Comedy? As soon as I heard that I was convinced that I was wasting my time. I don't think I'm funny at all. They handed me a script on the spot, it was a cold read, meaning I was just going to go for it then and there with no preparation. As the crowd all watched me, I took a deep breath, and told myself fuck it. Let's knock this out and get it done and over with so I can get out of here and not get stuck in traffic on the way home.

I gathered up my courage, started reading and to my surprise people started laughing. Was this a good laugh or a bad laugh? It was so weird. I hoped they weren't laughing at me personally, because that's not cool. Then I started to think, maybe they're laughing just to make me feel better while I'm doing my read. After all, it is a comedy right? As I continued to read the script, the laughing got louder and harder, and then I realized they were genuinely laughing at how good of a job I was doing delivering my lines. I had almost everyone there laughing! I was so shocked by how the audition went (in a good way), but even then I still didn't think much of it or that I would get the job. As I finished up and thanked everyone for the opportunity to audition, I walked out of the room and saw about 20 other girls waiting to audition for the same part. When I saw all these beautiful girls who were WAY prettier than me ready to audition, I figured it was a lost cause.

I headed home and didn't give it too much thought after that. A week went by and I never heard back from my agent about the job or the audition, so I had almost completely forgotten about it. Then one day, I got a call from my agent, and I remember in his distinct British accent saying, "Randi, you booked the Playboy TV show, well done." My agent was a very serious man that rarely smiled and he didn't put up with any shit from us girls, but when he told me I booked the Playboy TV gig, I could tell in his voice over the phone that he was proud of me. I think that maybe, just maybe, he even had a little smile when he told me I booked the job. I couldn't believe it! He gave me all the information regarding details about the job, and after I hung up the phone I jumped up and down I was so excited! I was going to be hosting my own show on Playboy TV! I had done a lot so far in the entertainment or adult entertainment business but this was a really big deal for me.

I'll never forget my first day on set for the show. As I pulled into the parking lot, they had a special parking spot right in front of the studio with my name on it. I had my own parking spot at Playboy studios! I felt like a total celebrity with just that alone but it got better. I had my own dressing room with my name on it. There was a huge bouquet of white roses on my table in my dressing room with a card from the producers and director welcoming me and congratulating me on the show. Not only that, but they also had a customized Playboy robe for me with my name embroidered on it and a bunch of other Playboy swag like a hat, t-shirt, and key chains etc. It was surreal. I had my own hair and makeup artist each day with a stylist and it was just a really cool set up for me. I was now contracted with Playboy TV. I loved working with Playboy TV, everyone there was so nice and cool and they had the best craft services (food for everyone on set). Oh and did I mention I got paid as well? The pay wasn't bad either! Other than the nudity it was just like working on a regular TV show. It was very nice, clean, and extremely professional. It was a really fun show to work on. I worked with Mary Carey (she was the porn star who ran for California governor), Jessica James, Jelena Jenson, Kaylynn, Steve-O, and Andrea Lowell to name a few. The show was called Totally Busted. It was an adult hidden camera practical joke series that ran original episodes from 2003-2006 and still to this day they air re-runs! I still get calls and texts from people telling me that they just watched me on Playboy TV. Shows and TV can be very interesting, and there are usually a few tricks that the audience isn't always aware of. Totally Busted had a few little secrets of their own to make the show run smoothly.

One of the dirty little secrets was that the majority of the show's cast had IFB's in their ear. IFB's (Interruptible Foldback or Interruptible Feedback) is a hidden earpiece that goes in the talent's ear. It provides a way of communication for the writers and/or producers to talk to the actors. In our case for this show it was used to feed us jokes and tell us what to say or do. It's a common practice especially for more candid "reality" type based shows. It also helps the director to tell you to move somewhere if you're blocking a camera. Since it was a hidden camera show, it's important to be able to see what's happening as much as possible since the cameras are already limited in their visibility. I don't think many people knew we had IFB's in our ear helping us along, but in my defense you still need to have some talent and a personality to go along with the show. If you can't deliver a line, or can't deliver a funny joke, it's just not going to work out or flow very well. Think about it for a moment, have you ever heard a really funny joke, but later when you try and repeat it, it just falls flat and isn't funny at all? A lot of jokes rely on the delivery. Not only that, but it takes a lot of multi-tasking to be able to interact with other people at the same time as receiving instructions or lines from a director talking in your ear. I remember they would give me instructions in advance or a line in advance in which case I would need to remember what to say and when to say it. It wasn't always the easiest thing to do but I really did love working on the show and we had a lot of fun.

That was one of our little secrets, another little inside bit of information most people don't know about is on the days that nudity was involved most girls didn't eat or drink water. It helped you look thinner on camera, and it also prevented you from becoming bloated for any reason. A lot of the girls also took diuretics or "water pills" to lose any excess water weight they may be carrying. Those were the mild versions of what the girls were doing in the dressing rooms. Some of the girls did cocaine, or got drunk especially if we shot late into the night. I personally didn't do any drugs on set but I did drink occasionally in secret with the other series regulars during long or late night shoots.

I loved doing porn but there are always pros and cons to doing anything in life. I thought it might be fun to share some of the gross things that happened to me while I was in porn. One day I had driven to set and most of our scenes were shot on location at really nice mansions, houses, or studios. This day I happened to be shooting at this big mansion and I had walked into the mansion and the second I stepped inside this huge place I was hit with this awful smell. It smelled like shit in this place. I had put my stuff down and got into the makeup chair to have my hair and makeup started for my scene and I told the makeup artist, "Man, it smells like shit in here." She replied with, "Yeah, I know they just finished shooting an anal scene before you walked in." I realized I was smelling ACTUAL shit. The worst part about it was I had to film my scene in the same place they had just finished shooting the anal scene, so it smelled horrible during my whole shoot. I had never done anal before, so I didn't know it but along with doing an enema before an anal shoot, you also aren't supposed to eat after a specific time and this girl must have broken that rule. SO GROSS!

Another gross thing is that I have had to go down on girls that have had really bad bacterial infections and they smell really bad. You have to try not to gag because cameras are rolling and you also have to pretend that you like it. It is SO GROSS! The thing about porn is that it was really easy for us to get bacterial infections and we got them all the time. Every time you get a bacterial infection you would have to take antibiotics for them. We had to be careful because when you take a lot of antibiotics, your body can get used to them and then your body can become resistant to them. But we were always getting infections; I got them often and I would douche because I would never want my vagina to smell ESPECIALLY if someone was about to go near it. Fun fact: dicks can smell really bad and most of the dicks that smelled were uncircumcised. Uncircumcised guys, if not kept super clean, can be really nasty. Sometimes they would have lint or built-up gunk inside when you pulled the foreskin down and it was GROSSSSSSSSSSSS because I not only had to smell it but I also had to put it in my mouth! And pretend like I liked it. I never said anything to these people because I didn't want to be difficult on set and I also didn't want to embarrass the people who smelled. I'd rather put a dirty dick in my mouth than embarrass the guy. I also didn't want the crew and director to wait around and be inconvenienced because I was being a "diva" on set. So I put the dirty dicks in my mouth because, after all, it was my job.

Another time I was on set and I was doing a boy/girl/girl scene and the other girl happened to be on her period. One of the tricks that porn girls do when they are on their period is they wet a makeup sponge or sea sponge, wring out the water so it is damp and then they stick it up their vagina to temporarily stop the bleeding so they can have sex. It works really well, you just have to make sure you take it out right after having sex because if you leave it in your vagina accidentally it can cause a bacterial infection. So this girl had a sponge in but she must have had a really heavy flow because when the guy pulled his dick out and I put it in my mouth, I wasn't paying attention, but then I tasted something funny and realized I just put a bloody dick in my mouth. Listen, I have done some nasty things in my life. I'm a gross ass bitch.

Another gross thing I had to deal with on set was girls or guys that were hairy down there and during a scene I would get a pubic hair stuck in my mouth or teeth and I couldn't get it out between takes and so I would just end up swallowing it. I also had to deal with guys doing a "cum shot" (when the guys cum on your face or body) and sometimes accidentally getting it in my eye. I would HATE getting a cum shot in my eye and that would happen quite a bit and it burns really bad. Every time it happened I had to pretend like I was enjoying him spraying a load of cum all over my face but really I was dying on the inside because my eye was on fire. I then would have to put Visine in my eye and have makeup touch my eye makeup up so we could take pictures with cum all over my face for the website pictures. It also put me at risk to get an eye infection. Also, when one of the actors farts and it smells, you have to try not to laugh.

An interesting dirty little porn secret is that some guys in porn would shoot their dick up with a drug (not sure what it was) to keep their dicks hard during the scene. I guess Viagra wasn't working for them anymore or it was something that worked better. I also had to have one of the male performers dig my sea sponge out when I was on my period when I couldn't get it out myself because my fingers weren't long enough. When he pulled it out it was full of blood and it was dripping all down his fingers and arm. It was gross. Sometimes girls squirt aka ejaculate and when they do, liquid comes out when they orgasm. Some girls do it, some girls don't. I was working with this girl who was known for squirting and it was my first time working with a squirter, so when we were shooting, she said, "I'm gonna squirt!" So I thought it would be a good idea to go down and catch it with my mouth. I went down and she squirt all over my face. Some of it also got in my eyes and it burned so bad I thought I was going to go blind. When I looked down at the floor her "squirt" was yellow! I was convinced this chick had just peed all over my face, but she told me after the scene that she had taken a lot of vitamins and that is why it was so yellow. Kinda funny, kinda gross. Another gross thing I had to deal with on set is that there was a girl I went down on that had vaginal warts! Genital warts are super contagious in case you didn't know. I didn't want to embarrass her so I didn't say anything on set I just cupped my hands over them so the camera wouldn't see them when we were filming. It was pretty gross but I also felt bad for her and wanted to help her. After the scene, I told her of a doctor that a lot of porn people saw to get treated for that. I ended up going with her to the doctor so she would feel more comfortable and wouldn't have to go alone. I watched her get her genital warts burned off.

There was another scene I did where I went down on a girl and she must not have cleaned herself before the scene because she had rolled up toilet paper in her vag and in her BUTT! That was gross because I was eating toilet paper because I didn't want to say anything because again, I didn't want to be difficult or embarrass her. I didn't end up eating the toilet paper from her butt area, because surprisingly I do have some limits. The grossest thing that ever happened to me on set was when I was fingering a girl and I felt something weird inside her. I ended up pulling out an old condom that got stuck up inside her. As I pulled it out it smelled so bad that I almost passed out. That condom must have been stuck in this chick's vagina for WEEKS!

CHAPTER 7

Private Jets and Private Islands

It was during this time while I was still shooting for Playboy and our shows were airing regularly that my old lawyer from my car accident from years prior had contacted me. It was a really random call because I hadn't talked to him since I was about 15 or 16 years old. I was now 18 or 19 and he said he was just calling to "check in" and see how I was doing. He also casually let me know during this call that he had just happened to see me on TV. That was when I realized why he was really calling me. Before we hung up he asked if I wanted to hang out with him sometime. He was much older than I was so at first I was thinking in my head, "Ummm, no."

But then he said these magic words about having a private island in Mexico, which he would fly out me and my friends to on a private jet. When I heard that, I thought it actually sounded pretty awesome. So I agreed to hang out and go with him on this trip. I ended up getting some of my porn friends together and we all ended up meeting at Van Nuys airport in the valley. When I got to the private airport, I realized my old lawyer, (let's call him Trojan) was going to be flying the plane we were taking to Mexico. That freaked me out, I thought to myself you're a lawyer, not a pilot! But to my surprise he had a pilot's license and flew himself all over to meet with his high-profile clients for work. He was a pilot and a lawyer. I came to learn that he was a much bigger lawyer than I had realized. I didn't really know much about Trojan other than he seemed like a really fun guy, and after talking to him for a while at the airport he was really funny too. He was like a big kid who was fun to hang around, when he wasn't being a lawyer. Trojan was in his early forties, overweight, and not attractive at all in my opinion so it's not like I was wanting to hook up with him, but he was definitely someone that I could see myself being friends with.

Once it was time to jump on the jet and head to our destination, I started to think this is freaking crazy. What if we crash? Small planes crash all the time.

Another porn girl and I getting ready to fly a private plane to Mexico

I started having really bad anxiety. However, as Trojan started up the plane and I listened to him talking to air traffic control, I started to feel a bit better. Trojan knew what he was doing. I found in my porn years that some people with money who own their own planes also have their license so they can fly themselves, especially if you were someone like Trojan who liked their privacy.

It was really cool flying with him for the first time because I learned so many things about flying privately. I smoked cigarettes at the time so we were able to drink and smoke cigarettes in the plane, which most people that don't smoke, they probably think that's disgusting but for people that do smoke that was like the coolest thing because you think, "Oh my God you can't smoke on a plane, that can be so dangerous," but back in the day people smoked on commercial planes all the time. We took advantage of that and were able to smoke and the other girls were doing all sorts of drugs on the plane on the way there. Even Trojan was drinking even though he was flying which definitely made me a little bit nervous. He wasn't drinking a lot but since I had almost died in a car accident with a drunk driver, and he knew about that because he was my lawyer in that case, he assured me by saying he could just put the plane on autopilot which I didn't even know existed until I heard about it. I mean, I had heard of it, but I didn't know it was an actual thing you did. He said once you're in the air flying and the weather is good you can just put it on autopilot and for the most part the plane will fly itself. He ended up putting it on autopilot and then came in the back to hang out with us! There was nobody up front flying the plane, there wasn't even a copilot or anything! That was definitely pretty sketchy but after getting a few drinks in me I wasn't scared anymore, my anxiety just melted away, and it just became a really fun flight.

That was probably one reason why I drank so much. I was just self-medicating. I had terrible anxiety and panic attacks that I suffered from daily since I was 17. Alcohol made my anxiety disappear until the next morning when I would wake up hungover and with even worse anxiety. So the cycle continues. My first time on a private jet turned out to be the most fun plane ride I've ever had in my life. It's not every day that you get to smoke and drink on a private plane. Trojan had also brought one of his friends with him who was also a pilot.

As we were approaching the island and getting ready to land, Trojan told us to look out the window. It was literally an island on the water with a little strip of dirt to land on and thank goodness I was drunk, because having a drunk pilot land on that strip was a panic attack waiting to happen. I had never been to this island before but it was definitely private. You had to fly in to get to this place. You couldn't drive to this house or property. When we got off the plane we were greeted by the staff and as we walked closer to the property I noticed there were helicopters, ATV's, dirt bikes, and basically every fun thing you can think of was at this place. It was like adult summer camp for rich people. I was wondering about the helicopters though, thinking to myself what do you need helicopters for? I found out later on why the helicopters were there but when we got there we kept being greeted by all the staff.

We walked into this massive, gorgeous mansion right on the water and it had a bunch of other little houses like wine cellars, maid quarters, and more. There was this huge chandelier hanging from the ceiling right when you walk in, and that same night Trojan was literally butt ass naked, drunk as fuck, swinging from the chandelier. It was in that moment that I knew our friendship was sealed. He was definitely my type of people. It was just one huge party and we were partying HARD. We had staff cleaning up after us, so we never had to clean or cook. They made us every meal. I don't remember how long we were there for, but at one point we went barhopping with a helicopter; we took a freaking helicopter to go bar hopping in Mexico!

Us in front of the helicopter we took bar hopping

There are clusters of islands that you can land on and drink all day.

Another day we got really drunk on a helicopter trip and jumped out of the helicopter naked into the ocean. I was so scared to do this, but I was super drunk so I did it anyway, and afterwards I felt like a total badass. I'm also terrified of the ocean so it was a big deal. I would have never done that sober.

My friends and I ended up taking those trips to Mexico probably once every two months. It was also fun for Trojan because when my friends got drunk, they liked to hook up with the guys. I later came to find out that both of the guys we went and partied with were married and had kids. Their wives didn't know. I think that it jaded me later on when I found out, but it happened so many more times throughout my porn career that it was just a common theme with married men. They would hire porn stars to hang out or sleep with and that messed me up as far as relationships and trusting guys went.

On another trip, they rented out this house in another area of Mexico and I got way too drunk that night, drunker than usual. We went out to a club and I was dancing around by myself in this club and somehow I cut my eye open really bad and I was bleeding down my face. Blood was everywhere and I didn't even know it. One of the girls looked at me and freaked out. She was like, "Oh my God are you okay!?" and I said that I felt fine and didn't know what she was talking about. I just kept partying with a full face of fucking blood. It's so crazy now to look back and think back to the life I lived.

That night, I remember that some local Mexican guy had broke into the house that we rented and was trying to rob us in the middle of the night. I remember the guys getting up and pulling out guns and it was this huge thing that was really scary. The next morning I had woken up and I had felt like a ton of bricks had hit me in the face. I walked into the bathroom to look in the mirror because my face hurt so badly. I was expecting to see a bruise but when I looked at myself in the mirror I scared the shit out of myself. There was a huge gash in my eye and my whole face was covered in dried blood. I jumped in the shower and cleaned my face up, but it hurt so badly. I woke up the guys and told them I had to get back to LA as soon as possible. They realized that it was a serious situation, since my job is based on how I look, and got us a flight within the hour. That is one of the perks of having your own plane.

On the way back to LA there was a really bad storm, and the guys got really nervous flying, which I'd never seen before. We had to make an emergency landing at a random Mexican airport because the weather got so bad. I had a full-blown panic attack in the air and the whole way down until we landed. Because of the sudden landing, the Mexican police ended up stopping us and wanted to search our whole helicopter and I thought they were going to stick their fingers up my butt.

I was paranoid because I hadn't done anal before and I didn't like things up my butt and it was just really creepy and scary. Everything was just going wrong on this trip. Of any moment to get stopped by the police, I had to get stopped when my face looked like I had been in a fight. It's just like the old saying goes: when it rains, it pours. I cut my eye open, we got robbed, our flight had to make an emergency landing, and now we were getting searched by the Mexican police. I just wanted to get home to my mom and more importantly, my plastic surgeon.

We waited for the weather to pass, eventually got home, and then I was finally able to see a doctor. It was super painful, but we got my eye all stitched up and I was good to go. The only problem was that I had an audition the very next day to do the cover and centerfold of Penthouse. They wanted to take some test shots of me for the cover and I had to go with my eye all in stitches and I'm pretty sure there's still a picture online somewhere from that test shoot with stitches in my eye. I never ended up booking that job, which is not surprising. It's safe to say I haven't had tequila since that time in Mexico.

Penthouse test shoot picture with stitches above my eye

CHAPTER 8

What Really Happens At AVN

During this time I was still shooting for Playboy and after talking to one of my porn friends about this recent trip, she asked me, "What's your rate?" I said, "What do you mean, what's my rate?" and she said, "Well you know, your rate for hanging out with these guys." I was a little confused, so I said, "What do you mean? They pay for the whole trip, they pay for all our food, it's like a free vacation and it's so fun." She said, "Randi, you're supposed to be charging for that." I was so confused and I didn't really know what she was talking about. After some explaining, I learned that there's this whole world of escorting in the porn world that I didn't really know about.

I was still super naive even though it felt like I'd been in the business forever. I was working almost every day and did not know about this whole escorting world for porn stars. I knew about prostitution because I had done that when I was younger but I didn't know that porn stars did that too. We already made so much money but then I found out I could make up to $50,000 per weekend just for hanging out with guys like my old lawyer. I didn't know if our guys knew this or if they had hired porn girls in the past, but it seemed like a whole new world that I was introduced to from this porn girl. I was able to sign up with an actual agency for escorting that I didn't even know existed, but this is not just your average escorting company; this is an escorting company for porn stars, Miss USA pageant girls, Playboy models, even mainstream actors that you see in movies and television. It was like a high-class escorting service and there were agents for it with a high-profile client database. The agency was similar to Heidi Fleiss's prostitution ring, and surprisingly, women mainly led the rest of the escorting industry.

The agency I worked for was one of the biggest in the business. They had a secret website that required $1,000 just to become a member and view the women. There were thorough background checks and all kinds of other things to make sure it was safe but it was a whole new experience. I thought the porn world was crazy, but this whole escorting world was like a whole other level of crazy because it was so private and secretive. You would be very surprised at some of the people that hire escorts...I know I was. It was everyone from professional athletes to really big politicians to celebrities and all kinds of very, very, wealthy individuals who either worked so much that they didn't have time for companionship, or they were married men who just liked to have fun and do things that they shouldn't be doing.

I turned out to make more money from escorting than porn, but I was still doing porn at the same time. The reason I was able to make so much money escorting was because I was doing porn, and these guys that had been watching my porn wanted to have that in real life. It was anywhere from $2,000 per hour, to weekend trips where I would spend the weekend with them and get paid thousands and thousands of dollars to be wined and dined and taken shopping. Some of these guys would let us buy whatever we wanted and take us all over the world. For me, it was an opportunity to meet smart people from all different walks of life. I learned a lot about business, about people, about culture and traveling, and I got to make a lot of money while doing it. Contrary to what most people think, most of the time was not about sex, it was just about your companionship and hanging out and talking to them. When we had sex, it would take 10-20 minutes out of the weekend, so the rest of the time I could learn about their lives, make them feel sexy and wanted, and provide them quality time. I became friends with a few of the men, and refer my friends to them. Sometimes they would book two or three girls together and it felt like one big party. Plus, I didn't grow up super wealthy so I never knew I'd be able to travel, go on yachts, or private planes.

After I'd been escorting for a few months, AVN came around. AVN stands for Adult Video News. It's basically like the Oscars for porn. They have a big awards ceremony and recognize the best actress, best new starlet, best 3-way scene, and other awards that porn stars may get. It takes place in Las Vegas and is a HUGE deal in the porn world. People from all over the world come to Vegas during this time to see the awards. It also always coincides with a business convention that people use as an excuse to take a trip the same weekend as the AVN.

Me at AVN

Signing autographs for Red Light District

Posing for porn paparazzi

Basically, a lot of them lie to get out there and see or interact with porn stars and there is a ton of escorting that goes on. I think the escorting is probably the biggest thing that happens during that time in Vegas. You can expect to make between $50,000 - $100,000 in a few days because of how many people want to book you. Some of these people are coming from very far away and so they're willing to spend a lot of money to see porn stars. As I said, this is a crazy event that even celebrities and professional athletes attend. At my second AVN, I had Ron Jeremy, Chuck Liddell, Victoria's Secret models, a bunch of porn stars, and five military guys in my room in full uniform.

Supporting our troops in my Vegas hotel room

I can't remember how they got to my room, but I do remember there was alcohol and cocaine everywhere. In general, AVN was wild, and people were really fucked up and did insane things. People were having sex in the open, and it was always a good time. In the following years, I would get my team (I had an assistant at the time) and I our own entourage of people; friends I would hang out with that weren't in porn but wanted to hang out with me because they liked my lifestyle. I would get us all matching outfits and matching pajamas for us all to roll around in.

Picture of me and my assistant

Some of the matching outfits we went out in

My friends and I in matching outfits

In matching robes in the hallway of our hotel in Vegas

We would end up drunk in the hallways of the Bellagio hotel, completely naked and not know where our clothes were. Once, a few military guys passed us in the hallway, and we asked to wear their clothes and they literally gave us their clothes. We ended up having a naked photo shoot in the hallway with these military clothes and then had to go downstairs in the giant man clothes to ask for a new key. Like I said, crazy things happen at AVN.

In the hotel hallway in some guys military uniforms

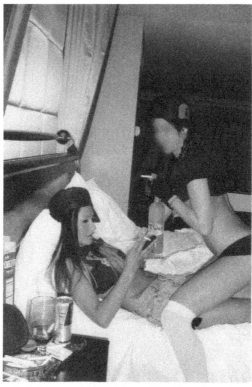

In my Vegas hotel room at AVN living off vodka, cigarettes, and Cheez-Its

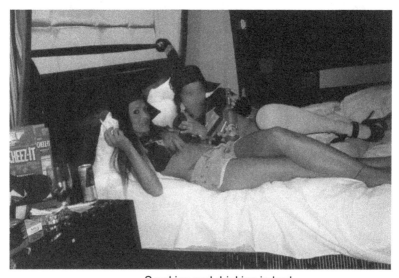

Smoking and drinking in bed

The Secret World Of High Class Escorting

Escorting is fun, but at the end of the day, it's a business. When you are escorting for high-profile clients, a lot of them make you sign NDA's, or nondisclosure agreements. It's a contract stating that you can't talk about the person or anything you see that could identify the person somehow. Basically, anything you do with them is a legal secret. I'm legally not allowed to name anyone who requested I sign one. Most of the trips with these men weren't trips where they could be seen out with us. Instead, we would be going to a non-disclosed location that we wouldn't know about until we arrived. All we were given prior to the trip was an address to meet at, where a driver or personal assistant would be waiting to take us to our destination The first time that this happened, I felt sure I was going to be murdered or sold as a sex slave, and it was one of the scariest days of my life.

It is definitely scary to show up at a random place and have no idea what to expect. Sometimes we ended up at the man's home, or at the home of his friend or somewhere else entirely. Often there would be parties going on or random people hanging out that you'd have to interact with and meet. Some clients had illicit rooms or areas of their house where they kept drugs, had sex, or held parties in. One man's home had a whole floor dedicated to drugs, where there were bowls of cocaine and drawers of ecstasy like a candy store. I remember asking the man if he was afraid that the cops would find out, like if a neighbor called for a noise complaint. He laughed at me! He said the cops were all paid off. It felt like the kind of conspiracy you only hear about in movies, but it wasn't a movie, it was real life. I realized that people with loads of money are really fun to hang out with, but you don't want to get on their bad side.

A few times I was really scared because I couldn't help but assume that if I pissed off this person, or if they're on drugs and something weird happens, that they may freak out and end up killing me. No one would find out what happened and even if someone did find out, it's unlikely that anything would happen to the person. Wealthy people run the world, and even though I never had any big issues with any clients, it was always on the back of my mind. Even now, I try to be really careful about not revealing any identifying information about my clients because I've gotten messages from them saying things like, "I better not be in that book." They have a lot to lose if I did name them, and I'm not trying to fuck with that. I have worked really hard for what I have in my life, especially my husband and beautiful baby girl. The last thing I want to do is piss off these people; it's just not worth it to me. So if you're wondering why I'm not saying specific names of these people, that is why.

Another interesting experience in the world of escorting are the lavish sex parties. Agents would rent out mansions, invite the girls, and clients could pay to attend. These happened every 3-6 months, and they would always take place at an undisclosed location. You wouldn't know the location until the day of or night of the party for safety and security reasons, so that random people couldn't find out where it was happening. The clients could enjoy the party and mingle, and when they found a girl they wanted to hook up with, they would ask that girl to one of the rooms. The party had custom poker-type chips, that the clients could pay for and they would pay the girls using the chips. At the end of the night, we could cash in the chips. These were all masquerade parties, so everyone was wearing masks and you often couldn't tell what people's faces looked like until you went in a room with them. All we ever knew about the clients was that they had to be rich, as the parties were expensive.

It was fun for us too, as the girls had their hair and makeup done, and got to wear beautiful gowns. The parties were very luxurious with ice sculptures, catering, a full bar, and entertainment. It wasn't only porn actresses at these parties, but also Playboy models, regular actresses, Victoria's Secret models, and just ordinary beautiful women who worked at grocery stores or the mall. People you wouldn't expect to escort do all the time, and they get paid extremely well. Escorting is a huge business that seems to fly under the radar of society, and includes everyone from cashiers to A-List celebrities.

The darker side of this business is the drug and alcohol use. It is everywhere. The girls are rarely sober at these parties, most of them drinking excessively, but some shooting heroin, doing lines of cocaine, or mixing pills. People would get pretty fucked up and at a few of these parties, there were paramedics onsite in case something happened. This was also to prevent news of the party from leaking out. If someone has to call 9-1-1 for an overdose, it could reveal things about people in attendance. So instead, paramedics were onsite to administer Narcan or emergency help in case it was needed. I once heard that a girl died in a room at one of these parties from asphyxiation. Nobody wants to take responsibility for something like that and when people's reputations are on the line, the right decision rarely gets made. I don't know the full story of what happened or if it was completely true, all I heard was that a body was found and left in a room from one of these parties.

I couldn't believe I had been in the business for almost two years before I found out about the escorting that goes on in the porn world. I was really curious as to why no one talked about it. I started getting heavily involved in high-profile escorting, but stories from that time could be a whole book on its own. After escorting for these clients, I soon realized why no one spoke about it. It is SO secretive that in the porn world, the girls won't even admit to each other that they are escorting as "side work." The only people that knew you were doing side work were girls who were hired with you for the same client at the same time. Side work was way easier than porn and often was way more fun. I ended up escorting more than I did porn most of the time. I even started booking girls for clients since I was so involved in everything. The men and women trusted me and so it worked out in everyone's favor.

One girl who I escorted with all the time was also a VERY popular porn star. Let's call her Messica. She was super cool but whenever she drank and mixed drugs she would get all kinds of crazy. I decided one year to bring her on a camping trip with my family. I made it very clear to her that it was a FAMILY camping trip and that we wouldn't be partying, just hanging out waterskiing, jet skiing, and camping. She really wanted to come so I invited her and her husband at the time. We went there for the 4th of July. I didn't think she would do anything crazy on this trip because she knew we were there with my family. The first two days of our trip went really well. We were all having fun and then the third day rolled around and she decided to get day drunk, which is when things started going down hill. I had taken a nap on a lounge chair and I got woken up by my dad telling me that I needed to check on my friend. I got up, turned around, and saw that she was banging on some random person's motorhome repeatedly. I quickly ran over to her and asked what she was doing. She told me she needed to go to the bathroom and she was locked out. I said, "Messica, that isn't our motorhome." She was convinced I was lying to her and that I just didn't want her to use the motorhome bathroom. She proceeded to keep banging on these poor people's door. She was clearly drunk and on drugs and was out of control. This girl is SUPER pretty so even when she wasn't making a huge scene everyone is staring at her. When she does do crazy shit, people cannot look away. I swear everyone in that campground was watching this go down. I apologized to the owners of that RV and finally was able to get her to our motorhome so she could go to the bathroom. I was so embarrassed.

Later, I got her to take a nap so she could sleep it off. She agreed and then fell asleep. Thank god. Around 6 pm, Messica wakes up. She comes out of her tent and starts drinking again. We just brushed it off and just let her do her thing. We are now all sitting around the campfire telling stories and cooking dinner. Then Messica decides she is going to get up and she starts walking towards our motorhome but she ends up walking right past it and into the campsite next to ours. I looked at her husband like, that is all you, go handle your chick, but he said, "No you go, she doesn't listen to me." Somehow I always ended up taking care of her. This time I stood my ground and said no. Her husband said she was fine and to let her do her own thing, so we went back to doing what we were doing. I wasn't too concerned because she was right next door to us. It hadn't been more than two minutes before some guy from next door came into our campsite and asked if we knew Messica. We said yes and he said she started peeing on the floor of his motorhome and asked if we could come get her.

These guys camping next to us probably thought they had scored with some hot porn star walking into their campsite in her bikini. Little did they know what was coming their way. I ended up apologizing again for her and running over to their campsite to get her. When I walked into their motorhome I found Messica with her bikini bottoms around her ankles squatting down in the middle of this guys motorhome, but she wasn't peeing. She was taking a shit. There was literal shit on the carpet floor of this dude's motorhome because Messica was so drunk that she thought in her mind she was in the bathroom. I then had to get her out of their motorhome, clean up her shit, literally, and again apologize a bunch of times to these guys. I was mortified. But the trip didn't end there, there's more. The next day, Messica went to take a shower at the public showers in the campground and she had been gone for longer than she should have. I got worried about her so I went looking for her. I looked everywhere and she was no where to be found. Soon everyone we knew was looking for her. We had been looking all over the campground for her and a lot of time had gone by. I was scared someone raped and killed her and we would find her body floating in the lake days later. We ended up calling the sheriff's department to help us search for her. I was crying hysterically and worried sick. Four hours had gone by and all of a sudden, Messica comes strolling into the campsite, fucked up, like nothing happened. I asked where she was and she casually said she went to take a shower. I have no idea where she really went, or where she was during that four hours but whatever drugs she was on caused some serious problems on that camping trip. These are the kinds of girls who partied with me through escorting and porn, and they were wild.

I didn't have too many bad experiences when I escorted but there was this one time that shit went terribly wrong. The bad thing about escorting with very influential or wealthy people is that if something goes wrong you can't really call the police because there's a good chance they are paid off by these men. People that have a lot of money have a lot of power. I was flown out on a private jet to spend a weekend with this guy in Miami, and everything was going really well. We were having a good trip, but at one point, in the middle of a conversation, the man got angry with me for something I had said. I asked if he was okay and that made him more upset. Apparently he didn't like how I was arguing with him about the point he made; maybe he wasn't used to people standing up for their opinions. All I know is it was like a different person came out. Shit escalated real quick. He started saying demeaning things to me, like telling me I was nothing more than a trashy porn star. I told him that I could leave if he'd like. He told me I wasn't allowed to leave because he paid for me for the whole weekend. He started making me feel really shitty and that is when I lost my cool. I told him I didn't care who he was and that I would leave if I wanted to.

This guy had some serious mental issues and they were coming out. We started screaming at each other and there was security outside the door of the penthouse because he was a well-known politician. I knew security heard us, but they never came in. I went into the room where all my stuff was and I started packing my clothes because I didn't want to spend one more second with this crazy guy. He asked where I was going and I told him I was leaving, that I didn't deserve to be treated that way. He said I wasn't going anywhere and that I would stay there as long as he wanted me to. My heart started pounding. This guy was supposed to be safe, he was booked and cleared through my escorting agency and at this point I didn't feel safe. I was scared. This guy came up right next to me and put me over his shoulder. I didn't fight it because I was confused and not sure what he was doing. He walked over to his balcony, opened the sliding glass door and took me outside. This guy lived on the very top floor in the penthouse suite. He owned the whole top floor of the building. He proceeded to dangle me over the side of his balcony threatening to drop me if I didn't listen to him. I started screaming, "Help he's trying to kill me!" I thought he was going to kill me and twist the story that I committed suicide. I screamed really loud and the guy never once got scared that someone would see what he was doing or have any repercussions for them. I peed myself I was so scared.

I knew security heard me but they never once came in to help me. I realized they were hired for HIM, not me. I didn't want to die that day. There were too many things I still wanted to do. I started praying and forgiving all my sins just in case he decided he was going to drop me. All of a sudden he pulls me back over the side of the balcony and calmly asks me if I learned my lesson. I wanted to punch him as hard as I could in his face but I was way too scared of him now so I just softly said, "Yes, I'm so sorry sir." I ended up having to stay there the rest of the weekend and he told me if I ever spoke about or told anyone what happened that he really would kill me the next time. I was so scared to escort with anyone new after that experience.

CHAPTER 10

A Marine and A Psycho

During this time I had met another porn star on set one day and she was my spirit animal…or so I thought. Her name was Katie. She was a tall, blonde, blue-eyed Barbie doll type girl with fake boobs and a gorgeous smile.

Katie and I

She seemed super cool and down to earth. It just so happened that she was looking for a roommate at the same time I was. I was considering moving out of the place that I was renting, mainly because I didn't like living alone and being so well known in porn I didn't feel safe alone in my house at night so I decided after the first day of meeting this girl that I was going to move in with her. The rent was cheaper than what I was paying and she seemed awesome so I thought it would be fun to live with her. Besides, we clicked quickly because we were living the same lifestyle. We both liked to drink and party, we both did porn and escorted and had similar schedules. Everything started out great when I moved in, it was almost too good to be true. We became best friends and did everything together.

Katie, another girl, and I

The scary thing about people is that you can spend every day with them and think you know them well but people can be really good at hiding things. I was also kind of oblivious to certain things and let a lot go because I try to see the best in people.

A few months had gone by and we were at home and Katie started acting a little weird. I had brushed it off and thought nothing about it, but it started happening more and more. That is when I started paying closer attention. One day I had knocked on her bedroom door because I wanted to ask her if she wanted anything from the grocery store. When I knocked on the door it just swung open because it wasn't all the way closed and I noticed that she was in the shower, so I walked into her bathroom that was in her bedroom. I didn't think she would mind since we did porn so it wasn't like she would get embarrassed if I saw her naked. But as I walked in I noticed that the shower was on but she wasn't in the shower, instead I found her sitting on her bathroom floor in front of the toilet fully clothed. I was shocked when I saw what she was looking at. As soon as she saw me she flipped out. Katie started screaming at me, "GET OUT, GET OUT!" She stood up off the bathroom ground and physically pushed me out of her bathroom so I couldn't continue to see what was going on in there. Katie had this whole mural of pictures cut out of me taped all over these poster boards and she was talking to them when I walked in.

It looked stalker-ish and creepy. I gladly walked out and she slammed the door behind me. I just thought to myself like okay, that was weird but I just left for the grocery store and figured we would talk about it later. When I got back home I sat down with her and just said, I am not going to judge you, I am open minded, but what the fuck is up with those poster boards? I think I made Katie feel comfortable with me and that she could tell me anything because she was my best friend, and I wanted her to feel like she could tell me anything. So she opened up to me and was honest about what was going on in the bathroom. She said they were her inspiration boards and she was praying to them. She said she wanted to be just like me and that she looked up to me. I was a bit taken back, a bit flattered, and a bit creeped out but I didn't want her to think I thought she was weird because I try to accept everyone no matter what. After all, we all have weird things we do, so I hugged her and told her I was flattered but that she was perfect just the way she was and that she shouldn't feel embarrassed or feel like she had to hide anything from me. I even told her we could do a collage poster board together one day to hang in our rooms of goals we had so she wouldn't feel bad about what happened that day.

I would always do my best not to judge all the weird things Katie would do, but the longer we lived together the more it started getting even weirder. We had gone on a trip to Lake Havasu with some of our friends who make portable stripper poles. For this trip, we had driven up to the lake in my hot pink lifted truck and we had one of their portable stripper poles in the bed of my truck. This was one of the many dumb ideas I had that drew even more attention to us. The last thing I was thinking about was my safety. I just wanted a cool car and to be popular.

The trip to the lake was on Memorial Day weekend and that is when a bunch of people go out to the lake and party on boats. It is like one huge party on the lake where people boat hop and get drunk. Our friends who owned the stripper pole company had a boat and there was a stripper pole in the boat. It was super fun because all the porn stars were drunk dancing on this boat with loud music coming out of the speakers and it was by far the most popping boat on the lake that year. Everyone was having a good time and then out of nowhere, Katie started getting really weird again but this time was a little different. I had noticed she kept getting off and on the boat over and over. I guess she was doing a bunch of cocaine and no one knew about it at first because she was hiding it so well. I was drunk so I wasn't paying much attention to her. I never saw her do coke before this trip. I quickly found out that when Katie did coke she got REALLY weird. We all kept telling her to slow down on the coke because she clearly didn't need anymore but she just kept doing line after line with no end in sight. She kept saying weird stuff like, "I just need a little more so I can be skinny like you Randi." I knew I needed to intervene at this point so our party on the lake that day got cut short and I told the guys we needed to take her back to the house we rented out there.

Katie was insecure about her self-image. I think she wanted to feel pretty and she didn't, although everyone else thought she was gorgeous and had a perfect body. Inside she felt like there were so many pretty people out at the lake that day and she wanted to look like them. I felt sad for her because she definitely had a mental illness that made it so she couldn't see how beautiful she actually was. It was heartbreaking. I mean, I had insecurities as well, but I think I internalized mine and dealt with them differently. Regardless of how she felt, I had to cut her off because she was not doing well and the last thing I wanted was for her to overdose.

We got back to the house later that night and I told her to lay down and try to let the drugs wear off. I gave her some food and told her to down a bunch of water. I left her alone in the room to chill out and then went back to hanging out with our friends who were also staying in the same house with us. Less than an hour later she went rummaging through everyone's bags and took everyone's drugs! She straight up stole prescription pills, weed, coke, and took all the alcohol she could find in the house. She grabbed anything she could get her hands on and then locked herself in the bathroom. Once we realized what she had done, I panicked because I thought she was going to try and take it all at once and kill herself. I was banging on the door and was getting ready to have one of the guys break it down until I heard her say that she was flushing everything down the toilet. That is when I realized she was having a psychotic episode. I kept apologizing to the guys that we went on this trip with because they went out there to have a good time and they ended up having some crazy stuff happen. I just kept telling them when she's sober she's really cool, but I was lying because even when she was sober she was a bit weird. I noticed that she had a lot of issues but so did I, so who was I to judge. I let her do her thing as long as she wasn't in danger. She ended up flushing all the drugs down the toilet so everyone's drugs and alcohol ended up down the drain. She kept screaming that if we were going to cut her off from doing more drugs, everyone else would have to stop too. She didn't want anyone else having a good time if she couldn't.

Even after that trip, she continued her strange behavior. I started to think it was probably best for me to get my own place again but I was scared to tell her because of how emotionally unstable she was, so I decided to stay. I really did want to move out though especially because in the place we were living, the neighbors hated us. We would have parties a lot and play loud music and we were just awful neighbors to have. I remember one day I had left the back windows of my truck open and somebody that did not like me put dead fish in my car through the cracked windows. It was the middle of summer so it was really hot. My truck had been sitting out there for a couple days with dead fish it. I remember opening up my car to get inside and when I opened it, I was hit so hard with the most AWFUL smell. My car reeked and I had no idea what the smell was or where it was coming from. I also should mention I have a fish phobia, a really bad one. I do not like fish, they freak me out. I won't even get in the ocean water because I am so scared one will touch me. So when I was looking around in my car for what the smell was I couldn't find anything. I went to look in the back seats in my truck and I saw a bunch of dead fish in the back of my car. I just about lost my shit. Who does that? I kept thinking, would a neighbor do this? Did Katie do it? Did a religious group do this? I still to this day have no idea who did it. I had to have the whole interior of my car completely removed and install new interior because that smell would not go away. It was so disgusting!

There was another time Katie had stolen some of my porn clothes and I would ask her about it and she would say no, she didn't borrow them but then I would notice her wearing them on set when her and I would be shooting a film the same day. I had the call time right after her and so when she was done filming, I saw her wearing my outfit she said she didn't borrow. And by borrow, I mean she took without asking and when I realized it, I asked her if she had it and she lied so she was stealing my clothes. It was just little things like that, that were really weird that she would do.

One night I had gone to a party over in Agoura Hills, right outside of the valley. One of my friends had invited me over and I had never been before so they were all new people to me. When we got there, I noticed there were a bunch of Marines hanging out at this house. I totally have a thing for men in uniform, especially men in military uniforms. Ugh, so hot! I spotted out this one guy who I thought was really cute. He was really tall, super buff, and kind of shy. He had brown eyes and brown hair with tattoos on his arm. I totally wanted to do him. I wasted no time and immediately went up to him and we started talking. I asked him how old he was, what he did for work, where he lived and just got to know him a bit. His name was Dustin and he was super shy which I thought was adorable. He was drinking a Jack and Coke and I was drinking vodka. I was always only drinking vodka, that was my drink. I drank it straight and at room temperature. I loved my vodka. Vodka made me have so much more confidence; without it I probably would have never had the courage to go up and start talking to the hottest guy at the party. Sober Channon would have felt all insecure and shy and would keep to herself thinking no guys would want to talk to her. But drunk Channon walked into a party and owned it. I would get everyone else way drunk to liven the atmosphere, turn up the music, and get girls to take their bras off and hang them off chandeliers or lampposts. It was what I did. If it wasn't fun, we would make it fun. That was one of my many mottos, and also "Party Naked." By the end of the night I was making out with this super hot Marine.

> "If it's not fun, make it fun."
>
> - Channon Rose

Dustin and I drunk at a party

After the party, he brought me back to his parents' house which wasn't far from the house we were partying at. It was 3 am so his parents were asleep, but as we pulled up I looked up at the house and it was this huge mansion. This humble Marine grew up in a mansion! We went into the house and I ended up sleeping in his room at his parents' house! The next day we woke up, went to breakfast and I started to really like him. A week later we were exclusively dating. Here's the kicker, he lived on a military base in San Clemente! That was a bit far. His parents and all his friends lived in Agoura Hills so he would go there on the weekends to hang out and party but during the week he lived on Camp Pendleton which is a military base for Marines in Southern California.

I would drive all the way to San Clemente which was over a 3-hour drive to go visit Dustin on base. You have to be put on a list in order to get into Camp Pendleton so I would roll up in my hot pink truck with a bunch of porn stars and we were not discreet. It is kind of intimidating too when you go through the gate at Camp Pendleton because there are military police checking your license plate and writing it down. They check your driver's license and it was always very interesting all the looks we would receive when we drove onto base. Just imagine a hot pink lifted truck with a bunch of hot slutty porn stars driving onto a predominantly male military base. Everyone would stare at us, guys would yell to try and get us to hang out with them and the attention and controversy we caused when we went there was crazy. I am still surprised they let us on base every time we went there.

One of the many drunk nights in the barracks

They would always tell us we weren't allowed to spend the night at the barracks but we always spent the night there anyway and would hide if any higher-ups checked the sleeping quarters. We'd always get so wasted there and then we'd go knock on a bunch of random doors that we didn't know. We would be naked when they open the door and we'd tell them to come party with us, basically just getting into a bunch of "Chananagins." That was my nickname because everywhere I went I caused trouble.

We were always doing a bunch of things that we weren't supposed to do. I also don't know how the guys never got in trouble for us. We always had so much fun on base. I was always impressed that the guys would drink until 4 am and then have to wake up a few hours later and do PT (personal training) where they would have to work out and run. They always did it on like 2-3 hours of sleep super hungover or still drunk. Those guys were badasses.

When I started dating Dustin I was still doing porn because he was fine with it at the time. Katie then started dating Dustin's bunk mate so it worked out well because we would both go to visit them a lot on base and then they would come back and visit us on the weekends. I still wanted to move out of Katie's place because she was still doing some weird stuff and since I was dating Dustin, I now wanted a place of my own. I then found a place in Valencia. I didn't know how to break the news to her that I no longer wanted to live with her so I told her that I found a nicer place in a better neighborhood and that I was moving. Somehow she ended up moving in with me to the new place. I was trying to get away from her but I am too nice and didn't have the heart to tell her no. She was like, "I want to move with you!" She was really attached to me, but not in a good way so when I moved into the new place I told myself I needed to have boundaries from her and start hanging out more with my other friends.

When I started doing this, she got really jealous. She didn't want me hanging out with other people. She was getting possessive. I remember coming home one night from a Halloween party and my friends and I had dressed up and had gone out to some different clubs in Hollywood. I had invited her to come out with us but she refused. She didn't want to go, so I stood my ground with my boundaries and instead of staying home with her I went out with my friends. That same night we all came home from the club and my friends were planning on spending the night at our house. But when we walked in to the house, Katie came out of her room right away and screamed at everyone, "Get out of this house right now!" She was really losing her shit and I was starting to lose my patience for her jealousy and possessiveness. I was drunk and finally lost it and yelled at her.

I explained to her that I could understand if we were being too loud and you wanted to sleep but don't try to kick my friends out as soon as they walk in the door. Needless to say things between Katie and I's friendship went downhill from there. I clearly set boundaries and let her know that she wasn't in charge of me or who I hung out with and that if she didn't like living here she could find a new place to live. She didn't like that and she didn't handle it well at all.

The next day she freaked out and started packing all of her stuff up to move out but along with packing her stuff she started packing some of my stuff as well. She must have thought she was going to steal a bunch of my stuff out of spite. Not only that but I saw her light a cigarette up in the house and she didn't even smoke. She proceeded to look me straight in the eye and then put cigarettes out all over the carpet.

When I thought it couldn't get any worse, she then started destroying the ENTIRE apartment. Her name wasn't on the lease so she wasn't responsible for any damages she caused. This was her way of getting back at me for hanging out with my other friends! I asked her so many times nicely to not break things. She broke all the bathroom mirrors, she put holes in the doors, she wrote FAKE FRIEND with lipstick all over the walls, it was nuts. I ended up having to call the police because she would not stop destroying my place and she was packing up my Louis Vuitton bags, and expensive shoes right out of my closet in front of me. She was trying to steal my stuff and pack it up in her boxes as she was moving. I kept telling her the police were on their way but she could care less. She went crazy. She broke the window in our kitchen and then we ended up in a fist fight because she took something she knew was very valuable to me, it was a family heirloom my mom had passed down to me that was my grandmother's who had passed away. Katie knew that it was very special to me. That is when I lost it.

I pushed her to try to get the ring back from her and she hit her head on the wall, which wasn't my intention as I was just trying to get my ring back. I tried to pry it out of her hands but she was pissed that I shoved her so she swung at me and then it was ON! She punched me in the face, my adrenaline kicked in, and it ended up as a huge physical fight. Keep in mind, Katie was much bigger than me, but I beat her ass and she was fucked up when I was done with her. By the time the police got there, her and I were a bloody mess on the floor rolling around fighting each other. The cops let her go since it was a mutual fight. They wanted me to pull out receipts for the things she had packed up that were mine, which of course I didn't have on hand, so Katie made out like a bandit with all my expensive shit. I was so pissed but I was able to get my grandmother's ring back, which is all I really cared about. I ended up having to get a restraining order on her.

She ended up putting a restraining order on me but I don't know why she felt threatened by me as I never did anything to harm her until she hit me. I think it was just as retaliation but that's how that ended and I actually never saw her again after that. Thank God, freaking psycho.

CHAPTER 11

My STD Nightmare

Once Katie moved out, things started to settle down a bit. Of course, my life can never be boring though, so the second that my life started to feel somewhat normal, something happened that would again change my life forever. A friend of a friend in the porn industry called me to do a boy/girl/girl scene. Normally, all of my scenes are booked through my agent but sometimes I would do a scene here and there that weren't booked through my agency. I wasn't technically supposed to be doing that for many reasons but what's the fun if you don't break the rules once in a while. So I decided I was going to go to this scene that my agent didn't know about, but again everyone has to be tested so it wasn't anything that I was too concerned about.

I showed up to the set and I saw a new girl that I've never worked with before. Something about the whole environment rubbed me the wrong way. I ignored my gut instincts that day. Everything seemed a little bit off but I just kind of went with it. We started rolling and I noticed that there was this super raunchy smell coming from this chick's vagina. I have smelled some raunchy vaginas, vaginas with bacterial infections, vaginas that hadn't been washed before a scene, and vaginas after they had worked out. Basically, I have smelled lots of vaginas but there was something about this one that smelt RANK! I couldn't do it. I was about to vomit. I thought, oh my God this is the worst smell I've ever smelled in my life. When you do a boy/girl/girl scene, the guy has sex with the other girl, then you suck his wiener, he puts it inside you and so forth. Well he didn't even need to get his wiener anywhere near me because as soon as they started having sex, I could smell it. This chick's vagina smelled like death. I was convinced something died inside her. During the scene when he took his dick out and put it in my face to put it in my mouth, I just couldn't do it. I had to stop the scene because the smell was so bad and even the guy was like "Oh my God." We kept looking at each other like, this is not good, she needs a douche.

He was getting ready to throw up and so was I. I had to call cut and I asked the girl to come with me to the bathroom because I didn't want to embarrass her in front of everyone. Even though I knew everybody on set could smell her because it was that bad. I'm pretty sure everybody in the room wanted to throw up. I don't know how she didn't smell it or if she just didn't care. I feel like anybody who has a vagina that smelly must give zero fucks about life. I took her in the bathroom and I discreetly asked her if she wouldn't mind douching because it smells down there. She was like, "Oh really? I'm sorry." She acted like she couldn't smell anything and almost gave me a look like I was acting high-maintenance for asking her to douche. She ended up douching and we went back to doing the scene. She still smelled terrible but it was a little more tolerable. It was by far one of the worst scenes I had ever done because of how bad the girl smelled.

A few days later, I started having stomach pains and I wasn't really sure what it was. I thought maybe I was really constipated. Or maybe I had a cyst rupturing, which I had before, but it was a different pain than that. I wasn't sure what was wrong with me but I knew I was in a lot of pain. I had cancelled all my scenes that week because I wasn't feeling good. My boyfriend Dustin was on deployment so he was going to be gone for a while and I was alone.

A few days later the guy from that scene called me and said he tested positive for gonorrhea and that I should probably go get tested just in case. He also said to notify anyone I had worked with after him, but thankfully I hadn't worked at all because I wasn't feeling well. If a performer ever tests positive for chlamydia or gonorrhea they are quarantined and given a shot. Once they have the shot, they wait over an incubation period, then test again and if the test is clean they can work again. AIM (Adult Industry Medical) is also supposed to contact anyone that has worked with those performers for them to go in and test to make sure they are clean. The last shoot I did was with the smelly vag girl and this guy. Everyone's test was clean at that scene and at all my scenes. I was always so careful to check and make sure that everyone's test was up to date; I would double check with picture ID. I definitely didn't think smelly vag girl had anything. I just assumed it was a really bad bacterial infection. I figured the guy must have gotten it from somewhere else, but to be on the safe side I went and got tested earlier. My test came back the next day and it was negative thank God!

Days and days had gone by and my stomach pain was getting worse and worse so I end up going to the doctor because it was so bad. I had to cancel another week of work. Something was not right. The doctor said I was fine and that I most likely was constipated. I knew something was wrong so I decided to make an appointment with an OB/GYN to get a second opinion because my stomach hurt so badly. The OB/GYN did a bunch of swabs and tests and everything came back fine. I was frustrated because I didn't know what was wrong with me, nor did the doctors.

A month or two went by and this pain was getting worse and worse. I was so sick I could barely get out of bed and I could barely walk. I couldn't even eat I was in so much pain. I didn't know what to do. I had gone to two different doctors, and I had been tested and everything looked fine. I decided to call back my OB/GYN and let them know that something was wrong; that I was unable to walk because of the amount of pain I was in. I asked if they could please check me again. They got me in the same day and as soon as the doctor swabbed me and took my vitals he asked his nurse to call an ambulance for me. He said they were going to send me to the emergency room. The doctor looked concerned and said I had a really bad infection. I started freaking out, I had a really high fever, I could barely walk and I knew I was sick but I didn't realize how bad it was. I went to stand up to try to walk to the gurney for the ambulance from the doctor's chair and I almost passed out. The nurse ripped off some smelling salts off the wall and put them under my nose and it woke me back up pretty quick. The ambulance took me from my OB/GYN's office to the emergency room to have me admitted and treat the infection.

I guess I was close to dying. I got to the emergency room and I was all by myself. I was freaking out because I still did not know what the hell was wrong with me other than I had an infection. I didn't talk to my mom that much around that time. My mom knew that I wasn't feeling good and having stomach pains but she didn't know it was this bad. There I was, alone in the emergency room with my legs spread open as this ER doctor swabs my vagina. He pulled out the swab and showed it to me and it was SO gross! It looked like snot on an oversized Q-tip. He said, "This is the worst case of gonorrhea I've ever seen." I said, "What? I don't have gonorrhea, I get tested every month for it, I do porn and my test came out clean." He said, "Well they must have missed it because I don't need to test you to know that this is gonorrhea." He told me I was really sick and that I was going to have to stay in the hospital on IV antibiotics for the next few weeks. I was mortified! I was too ashamed to tell any of my friends or family so I stayed by myself in the hospital for weeks without anyone knowing. The staff there treated me horribly because of why I was there. I felt like a caged zoo animal. I heard the nurses whispering in the hall in front of my room and peeking in to see the porn star who almost died from a horrible case of gonorrhea.

I soon found out where I had contracted gonorrhea from and it wasn't the guy who called me telling me he had it. You remember smelly vag girl? She didn't have a bacterial infection, she had gonorrhea! Somehow she faked a clean test so she could shoot. I remember the doctor telling me that it was a possibility I could have some fertility issues from this. At the time that was the last thing that I was thinking about so I just wrote it off. I just didn't want to die. I was really sick and if they didn't treat me I could have died. It had been left untreated for months. Even after going to multiple doctors no one could figure it out until it wrecked my insides.

Once I was all better and out of the hospital, I was ready to get my life back on track. I hadn't worked in forever so I was trying to get my check from my last shoot because I still hadn't been paid. The whole thing was a really shady ordeal. I never ended up getting paid from that scene and I got gonorrhea. Those are some of the reasons why you're supposed to book things through your agent and not on your own so that you don't get screwed over like that. I realized that when I was tested, it was only a few days after that shoot and that the STD wasn't in my system long enough for it to register on my test. I haven't told very many people about getting really sick with gonorrhea because I was so ashamed about it. In an earlier video when I first started on YouTube, I talked about porn and said that I had never gotten an STD because I was really ashamed of it. No one wants to admit that they got an STD. I hope that instead of judging me for getting an STD that you can learn from my story. I thought it was important to share it with you because I don't want you to make the same mistakes I did.

CHAPTER 12

The Panty Snatcher

You're probably wondering where my Marine boyfriend was at the time and he was actually gone for training so I didn't see him during this time. I am so thankful for that because I didn't have to worry about passing that on to him. When Dustin got back things got more serious between us. I ended up moving into a different apartment called The Summit, which was in the valley. It was closer to work and a place where a lot of porn stars and celebrities lived.

A lot of famous people lived there because it was one of the only really nice gated communities in the area. I would have huge parties and always get noise complaints or security showing up at my door. I was always getting in trouble there. One night I remember we had a really big party and there were a bunch of Marines who had come to party from Camp Pendleton for the weekend and it was a HUGE party at my place. We were all really drunk that night and we accidentally forgot to shut our garage so it had been open all night. We had kept all my porn clothes, costumes, and lingerie in the garage because I lived with another porn chick at the time. All of our clothes and costumes were all hanging on clothing racks in the garage.

The next day we had noticed that some of our underwear were missing. The other porn chick that lived with me had a shoot that day and was looking for a specific outfit and noticed it wasn't there but we didn't think anything of it. The next night again we had accidentally left our garage open because we were drunk and irresponsible. When we went into the garage the next morning we checked to make sure nothing was missing and we realized the only things missing were our UNDERWEAR! Someone was stealing our fucking panties! We had this ongoing joke with my boyfriend at the time and some of our other Marine friends that we had a panty snatcher.

A few weeks later we were all partying again at our place and as always leaving our garage open on accident. Guess what? One of the people partying at our house caught the panty snatcher in action! The panty snatcher had creeped into our garage and was caught sniffing our panties and putting them in his pockets! This Marine partying at our house had gone outside to his car to get cigarettes and had seen the panty snatcher in our garage. Because this had been an ongoing thing and we had been talking about it and joking about it, the Marine ended up beating the shit out of this guy. He beat him up so badly that there was a blood trail from the inside of our garage all the way to where the panty snatcher lived. We didn't know it at the time but the panty snatcher lived in the same complex as we did. We had heard about what happened but we didn't know that all this happened the night before. The Marine never told us he beat him up. We were all drunk and for these Marines, fighting was just a common occurrence to them so it wasn't a big deal.

The next day he ended up telling us about it and we were like no way! We didn't believe him, so we went downstairs and saw this blood trail. We followed it to the panty snatcher's house and confronted him. The guy was really apologetic and said he didn't remember anything. He said he had started these new pills the doctor gave him and after a few glasses of wine he would forget the whole night and that he was really embarrassed. It never happened again after that. But what did happen after that was a lot of really good parties at my place.

At one party we all got drunk (surprise, surprise) and decided it would be fun to punch holes in all of our walls and doors. Everybody at the party was punching holes in the walls and within 10 minutes our whole house looked like a construction zone. I wonder where all my porn money went... to fix dumb shit I did when I was drunk. That same night someone clogged a sink downstairs and left the water running and somehow the washer also broke so when I woke up the next morning my whole downstairs was completely flooded. I looked around and there were people half-naked passed out all over my house, in my bathtubs, my front door was wide open and someone was passed out on my front porch. To an outsider, I was living in nonstop mayhem. But to me it was just another day.

CHAPTER 13

Getting Arrested

"When I do good, I feel good. When I do bad, I feel bad.
That's my religion"
- Abraham Lincoln

I was living with a different porn chick at the time who was cool at first, although it seems they are always cool at first. As I mentioned previously, when you do porn you get tested all the time and the porn chick that was living with me was new in porn. I took it upon myself to help teach her everything I knew because I remember how foreign everything was to me when I first got into porn and I wish someone would've helped me figure things out. I made sure to let her know how important it was to not sleep around and have unprotected sex because it could not only hurt other people but she would no longer have a job. Since she lived with me I was able to see a lot of the things she would do and how she acted with other people. The more I got to know her, the more I realized she was really selfish and was definitely not being smart about having sex when she partied. I started to see that this girl wasn't a very good person so I stopped wanting to hang out with her as much but we still lived together so when we had parties we would hang at the house together. She would sleep with all these random dudes and wasn't using protection and it pissed me off because it put a lot of performers who she could potentially work with in danger. I liked to party too and was at times very irresponsible, but I was never irresponsible about the important things like protecting myself and others in our industry.

I knew with the amount of people she was sleeping with that she was bound to get something. Lo and behold, she tested positive for chlamydia. She came home one day crying, and told me she tested positive for it. I was so disappointed in her especially because I had warned her about sleeping around unprotected with so many different people. I told her she needed to go to our special porn doctor to get the shot that makes the STD go away, that she needed to call and tell our agent and inform him about testing positive, and have him cancel her upcoming scenes. She said she would do all that but she just wanted to be alone the rest of the day.

A few days later, we were having another wild party at our house and she was super drunk and came up to me and said, "I still did my scene the other day." I said, "No you didn't." She said she got away with doing a porn scene while having an STD. I guess her test still had two days until it expired so she was still technically able to shoot because the stupid person working at AIM never called to put her in quarantine. I FLIPPED out. I started throwing and breaking shit (I was drunk). I started screaming at her and telling her she was a dumb bitch. Everyone at the party stopped what they were doing, got quiet and just stared at the drama that was happening between two drunk porn stars. I had so much rage inside of me because whoever she worked with most likely would contract it, and then that person works with someone else and then it spreads like wildfire in our industry. When that happens the trail always leads back to the one person who tested positive first and knowingly worked with an STD. That person is shunned in porn and no one books them anymore, and their career is over. It also made me look bad because I was helping her out and she was living with me so people would associate us together. I remember one person who everyone found out worked with an STD and the guy ended up moving out of the country to Thailand.

We are in the middle of this party and she was being such a bitch to me. I kept telling her how fucked up it was that she did that and she just looked at me and said, "Oh please, I got my shot, it's totally fine. Besides, I needed to pay rent." She then started laughing as if it was a joke and funny. I couldn't resist punching her as hard as I could in her face. Once I took that first swing I couldn't stop. I was drunk and I just kept hitting her over and over until someone eventually pulled me off of her. When I was pulled off of her I looked around and there was blood everywhere. It looked like a murder scene. There was blood all over her face and her blood was all over my face. I had broken her nose in a fit of rage. It was very wrong of me to do that, I should have never done that but being drunk and that upset it was a bad combination. I made sure to call my agent that night and let him know that she tested positive and to let the performers know that she worked with to get tested. After that, she was never allowed to work in porn since she KNOWINGLY worked with an STD. It was a bad night. She started crying and she left and stayed at a friend's house and I was like she's not living here anymore. I can't stand her. I didn't like her anyway and she was just bad people.

This is where the story gets good. I am passed out naked in my bed and it's probably 7 am the next morning. We left the door open because there's always a ton of people coming in and out. Since my door was open the police let themselves into my house. The police officers probably had no idea what they were about to walk into that day.

I am sure that when they walked into my house there were drunk people passed out all over. I wouldn't be surprised if they had to walk over people to get to my room. I woke up that morning to three or four police officers in my room. The police made me put clothes on and put me in handcuffs. They told me I was under arrest for assault and battery! This porn chick went to the police and ratted me out! I couldn't believe her. I was also SO hungover. She printed out one of my porn pictures of me naked to give the cops so they could identify me at my house to arrest me. I had to sit in a holding tank for hours super hungover with no food or water until I was able to be released. I was lucky enough to hear she had dropped the charges so I didn't have to worry about staying in jail or it going on my record, but it still sucked. I did feel really bad the next day even though I was pissed she called the cops on me, so I apologized for beating her ass. I never talked to her again after that.

Lessons I've learned:

- Even if someone deserves to be punched in the face, don't do it. It is not worth going to jail over.

- If you do end up hurting someone emotionally and/or physically always apologize after the fact. You will never feel good for hurting another. My mom always taught me two wrongs don't make it right. Just because someone does something wrong to you doesn't mean it is right for you to do something wrong back to them. Always be the bigger person.

CHAPTER 14

My First Marriage

A little more time had gone by and I ended up getting even more serious with Dustin. I fell in love with a Marine. I decided that I was going to quit doing porn, again, for another guy. I moved hours away, again, to live near my boyfriend and I ended up moving into an apartment right next to Camp Pendleton. I had saved up enough money to be able to move and put myself through school and if you guessed that I wanted to go to a different school this time around you guessed right. This time I wanted to go to nursing school. A few months after I had moved to be closer to Dustin, something NUTS happened! He came home one day from work, walked in the door, gave me a ring box, and said, "Will you marry me?" It was the most unromantic thing ever. He didn't even get on his knees. I don't think he asked my parents' permission, and it was really out of the blue, but I didn't care because I loved him. I said yes and that was it, we were engaged! I was so happy. I was also so young.

Engaged to a Marine and wearing his dog tags around my neck

Marine Corps Ball, and engaged (I also tattooed his initials on my ring finger)

I had thought that we would wait until his final deployment for us to have our wedding, so I would have plenty of time to plan it. After talking about it for awhile we decided to go to the court to get married and have the wedding when he got back from his deployment a year later. We did this because we would both get benefits once we were legally married. He would get paid more, he could have an allowance for living off base in his own apartment with me and I would also get health insurance. I also decided during this time that I wanted to get my phlebotomy license and I worked as a mobile phlebotomist for a while. Then I got my EMT license and that didn't work out very well. I ended up getting fired as an EMT and I got fired as a phlebotomist. It was really hard for me to have "normal" jobs after doing porn but I did try.

There was one night when a bunch of Dustin's military friends had come over to our apartment off base from Camp Pendleton, which they did often, but this night things went too far. I had gotten into an argument with one of his friends and we were all super drunk. I think one of his friends had made a vulgar comment to me about something that set me off. I ended up asking him to leave and he refused to leave. We ended up in an intense argument and I was screaming at him, "Get the fuck out of my house!" Dustin started yelling at me for yelling at his friend and I was pissed at everyone and felt like they were teaming up on me. I went into my bedroom and I slammed the door. As I slammed the door, the guy I was arguing with threw a remote control and it went through our cheap door and hit me in the back of my head. I was screaming at Dustin to get him out of the house. We were all really drunk and everyone ended up leaving and Dustin was mad at me for making all his friends leave. We were still arguing after everyone left and then I got so mad at him that I told him to leave too.

Dustin being Dustin

My little drunk ass was trying to boss around all these drunk Marines. These guys were pretty violent; they would beat up people at bars for fun. They liked to drink and they liked to fight.

Dustin and his friends drinking

That was their thing. I must have said something that set Dustin off. I can't remember exactly what I said because I was drunk and blacked that part of the night out, but before I knew it Dustin was dragging me by my hair from the living room to the bathroom. I thought he was going to try to kill me. He proceeded to lift the toilet seat up and then he lifted me by my hair and slammed my head into the toilet. I started kicking and screaming trying to get him off of me. I was freaking out. He finally lifted my head out of the toilet and asked me if I was done arguing with him. I was scared but I still spit in his face because I was so pissed. He shoved my head back in the toilet and into the water and was holding me down so I couldn't breathe. I thought he was going to drown me to death. He was 6'2" and extremely strong. He was also a Marine; they are trained to kill and he was trying to kill me. I was choking on the water and then he finally pulled me back up and threw me against the bathroom wall. He told me I was lucky that he didn't kill me and then walked out, sat down on the couch and turned the TV on like nothing happened. He then opened a beer and started drinking some more. I was really drunk so I couldn't drive anywhere and the only friends I had there were all his friends, so I slept in my car that night because I was too scared and upset to stay in the same house with him that night. There were a few times Dustin was abusive when he was drunk, but he was the sweetest person when he was sober so I stayed with him. I thought that is what I deserved and that no one would treat me well because I used to do porn.

I decided it would be a good time to go back to school since Dustin would be going away on deployment. I was interested in studying abroad so I ended up finding a nursing school in Saint Kitts that looked solid and decided that I was going to go there. It was out of the country and the first time I would be studying abroad. The school was called the International University of Nursing. It was an American-based school but located on an island. I thought it was so neat to be able to go to school on an island and I was super excited. I did a bunch of research on the school, but it was new so there wasn't too much information about it. Their website had pictures and it looked state of the art. I had never been to this island before, but it looked beautiful. They had really well-educated professors at the school and it wasn't easy getting accepted there. You had to pass all these tests, write an essay, and get your other degrees approved. I also had to complete an entrance letter. I studied hard to be able to pass all the tests. I spent countless hours working on my essay and entrance letter until it was perfect. I sent everything in and got a call a week later letting me know that I was accepted!

They sent me a welcome packet in the mail and I told my mom I was going away to college to study on an island. I wanted to get there two weeks prior to school starting so I could get acquainted with the area and set up my dorm room. I hoped to meet some kids at the school so it wouldn't be awkward on the first day not knowing anyone. I packed up all my stuff and my whole family went to the airport with me to say goodbye. They were all super supportive. I got on my plane and headed to Saint Kitts in the West Indies. It is part of the Caribbean near Jamaica and the Bahamas. It is one of the tiny islands around that area.

After a long flight, I finally arrived in Saint Kitts. I was exhausted. All I wanted to do was get to my dorm room and pass out. As I walked out of the airport, I was greeted by a man who drove up in this really dinky car. To be honest, I was pretty sketched out. It didn't look like he was from the school

I saw online. It is not that I cared about driving in a beat-up car, it just seemed like some random dude was picking me up. It didn't match up with what I was expecting, like an official school van or car picking me up. I asked him again if he was from IUON and he said yes, so I just went ahead and got in the car. He loaded my bags in the back and we were on our way.

As we were driving, I was pretty scared because I was all alone in another country. I had arrived later in the afternoon so it wasn't dark yet, but the sun was going down and as we were driving I noticed we were not in the best area. I was looking out the window and seeing abandoned houses. I started to freak out a bit because this was nothing like what I saw in the pictures online. It felt like a whole different island. The houses were all condemned and had graffiti on them. Between the car picking me up and now driving through a deserted neighborhood, I started to think this whole thing was a scam! These people are going to kill me and harvest my organs to sell on the black market! I was not in an official school vehicle, the guy driving me was a local and I didn't see a school anywhere. I asked the driver, "We are on the way to the campus, right?" He replied, "Yeah." But there was definitely a language barrier. All of a sudden, the car stopped. We are in front of some random house and he starts to get out and unload my bags. I panicked because this was not the school. I told him, "No, I am supposed to be staying at the dorms on campus." He told me, "They are not ready, you'll stay here." I thought that I was about to die. This is the house that they are going to kill me in and steal my organs. I didn't know what to do. There was no negotiation with this guy.

He seemed to be in a rush to drop me off so he drove away and I was standing outside of this random house with all my bags. I was so jet lagged and tired and all I wanted to do was sleep but now I was in this nightmare. I was young and dumb and didn't set up my cellphone to work on the island. The school's website said I would need to purchase a phone on the island. I slowly walked into this house and I was waiting for someone to come out from the shadows with a knife and tie me up. I kept looking at my phone praying that it might work and I could call for help, but it said no signal. I realized there was no school there and the whole thing was a set up to get me into sex trafficking or to sell my organs. I thought my life as I knew it was over. How could I be so dumb to get myself into a situation like this? I should have at least visited the school before coming here all alone.

I walked through this dark house and started flipping every light on. I was so exhausted and figured I was going to be killed soon so I at least wanted to try to sleep. Maybe if I went to sleep, I would be killed in my sleep and it wouldn't be so bad. This was my fucked up mindset. As I walked through the house, it smelled funky. I figured they must have killed people before in this house. Maybe this is what death smells like. You don't think straight when you are that tired. I found the nearest bedroom in the house and lifted the comforter to get inside the bed and when I saw what was in this bed I instantly started crying. The bed was swarming with ants. That was the breaking point for me. I ran out of the house and to the nearest neighbor to ask to borrow their phone. Thankfully, the neighbor let me in, probably because I was crying, and they let me call internationally to my mom. I was able to reach my mom and I was bawling to her telling her that it was all a scam and there was no school and that I thought they might be trying to kill me because they dropped me off at this random house and there were ants in the bed. I probably freaked out my poor mom but she helped calm me down and told me she would book me a room at a hotel on the island. There was one hotel on that island and thank God because I was not trying to stay all alone in the ant-infested house that smelled like death. I took a taxi to the Marriott on the island and was shocked when we drove up. It was the nicest Marriott I had ever seen. It may as well have been the Ritz Carlton. I walked in and felt SO much better. I got into my hotel room, it smelled nice, and the bed was super comfortable. I ordered room service and was SO grateful that my mom helped me get somewhere safe.

The next day my mom was able to get a hold of someone that worked at the "school" and they apologized for the inconvenience and said that the dorms weren't ready. The school was new and they would be done in a few days before school started back up. They explained that all the students had gone home for break. It made sense, it was a private school and there weren't as many kids going to school as you would see back home at a state college. That is why I didn't see any other students around. I ended up staying at the hotel for two weeks until the dorms were ready. Once the dorms were ready and school was about to start back up, everything was fine. The school was actually really nice and just like what it looked like on the website and I did get a great education there. Going to school abroad was a huge culture shock for me. I realized how sheltered I had been. I had traveled out of the country before, but I always stayed at fancy hotels or the good areas of the country. I had never experienced what it was like to live in a developing country. You see it on TV or in movies, but I didn't realize it was really like that. I thought they just exaggerated things for entertainment purposes.

When I first got to the island and was driving through what I thought was the ghetto, that was how majority of the island lived. It was heartbreaking. The grocery stores were infested with flies and had chickens walking around in it. Their hospitals were the same way. I didn't realize how ignorant and privileged I was until I studied abroad. I did a lot of volunteer work while I was there, teaching elementary school kids basic math and English in my free time. A lot of the kids would show up to school with little to no food some days, no shoes, and would be sick a lot. I would always bring peanut butter and jelly sandwiches for all the kids in my classes and buy as many shoes as I could and fresh water. I would cry every day on the way home because I wanted to stay with them and make sure they were fed. It made me have a newfound appreciation for my life back home. I ended up dropping out of that school only after one semester because I got island fever and needed to go back home. But I was so grateful for being able to have that experience and I learned so much, not just about nursing but about life and how some people are born into easy circumstances with many resources, and other people who are just as kind and deserving are born into hard situations.

CHAPTER 15

Another Baby Gone

After moving home, I settled back into normal life while Dustin was away.

Dustin on deployment

Dustin finally got back home from his deployment and we were still together, happy, and planning our wedding. One day I realized I hadn't gotten my period in a while, so I went to the store and got a pregnancy test. I went home right away and took it while Dustin was at work. I stood over the test until I watched blue lines appear on the test... OMG, I was pregnant! I couldn't believe it. You would think from what happened last time I got pregnant that I would be scared but I was actually really excited. I thought because we were getting married, he would be happy about me being pregnant.

Besides, I was paranoid because I thought that after having gonorrhea that I'd never be able to have kids or get pregnant. It was a total surprise. That day, I waited patiently for him to get home so I could tell him the good news. When he got home from work, I sat him down on the couch and told him I was pregnant. The look on his face instantly broke my heart. He put his hands over his head and said, "Well that's not good." I couldn't believe that this whole pregnancy cycle was happening to me yet again. I felt like I had some sort of pregnancy curse. I didn't understand. We were in love, and we were technically already married even though we hadn't had our wedding yet. If he loved me enough to want to marry me, why would he be upset about me being pregnant? He had even told me he wanted kids with me. I was so upset.

I left the house in tears and called my mom (My mom was and still is my rock). I just wanted to be comforted. I also figured that because I was older, she would support this baby, but she told me that I was still too young to have a baby and that I didn't have my shit together yet. She didn't think I was ready, the same situation as before. She muttered those words that crushed my heart, "You need to get another abortion Channon." I couldn't do that again. I felt like I was in a better situation now to be able to take care of a baby. I was a little bit older. I thought this had happened for a reason, so I refused to get an abortion. Dustin wouldn't talk to me because he also wanted me to get an abortion. I knew how horrible it was going through it the first time that I couldn't bring myself to do it again. I never got over the first time I ended my pregnancy and I never will.

I felt so alone and didn't have any support. Could I have this baby on my own and take care of it? Was Dustin going to leave me if I kept the baby? So many thoughts raced through my mind. I was lost and terrified. A few days later, I reluctantly caved into these thoughts and made an appointment at Planned Parenthood. I cried every day and felt like a piece of shit for doing this not once, but twice. I was sure to go to hell. It was the hardest day of my life getting in the car that day and driving to that appointment. Dustin and my mom went with me and I would like to say they were there to support me, but it felt more like they wanted to make sure I followed through with the procedure. As I walked up to Planned Parenthood, there were all these protesters and people outside yelling at me and holding signs of dead babies. They would yell at me that I was going to hell for killing my baby.

I was already distraught and broken about having to do this, and the protesters made it worse. I walked into the building in tears and couldn't stop crying. I didn't want to be there. I didn't want to be doing this. I wanted that baby. I knew I would regret it. I sat in the office waiting for them to call my name. Finally, my name was called and I went back into the room. They gave me an ultrasound to make sure the baby wasn't ectopic. They told me to take some Motrin and wait in this hallway for my procedure. I went to sit in the hallway and waited to be called into another room to have my procedure done. It was still early in my pregnancy so I didn't have to go under anesthesia or anything like that. Something inside me told me not to go in that room, so I got up and left. I couldn't do it. I walked out into the waiting area and my mom said, "All done?" I told them I couldn't do it and that I wanted to go home. They were both so disappointed in me. I didn't care. I wanted this baby.

My mom and Dustin said if I didn't want to do it today that it was fine, but that I needed to go within the week. I cried hysterically the whole way home because I knew I would eventually have to give up this baby. My mom and Dustin convinced me of all the reasons why it was not just best for me, but also the baby. By the time I ended up making another appointment for Planned Parenthood, I chose to be put under, even though I was still in the first trimester. I went to the building and still didn't want to go through with it. I was crying the whole time. Before I knew it, I was put to sleep. I remember being really out of it when I woke up, but it was over quickly. My pregnancy was gone. This experience was nothing like the first time with a private doctor. This place was more focused on seeing as many women as possible compared to the private doctor. They were trying to get me up sooner than they should have and I collapsed since the anesthesia was still strong in my system and I wasn't completely awake yet. They had to put me in a chair and I ate crackers and juice to get my blood pressure and blood sugar back up. I finally was okay to leave and just remember feeling depressed and horrible physically and emotionally for weeks afterwards.

I ended up getting a job as a receptionist to put myself back through nursing school and I just remember having these horrible cramps and bleeding. It felt like the worst period I had ever had. I called my mom from work and told her I felt sick and that I couldn't stay at work. I was still living in San Clemente and she was hours away. I was in so much pain that I couldn't drive myself from work to home so I called a taxi. They didn't have Uber or Lyft back then. She also said I should call Planned Parenthood and tell them the symptoms I was having and see what they say.

I called Planned Parenthood from work and they said it didn't sound good and to come in right away so they could take a look. I started getting nervous and went into having a full-blown anxiety attack. I told my work I needed to leave for the rest of the day and that I wasn't feeling well. I went to the same Planned Parenthood that did my procedure and the doctor that was looking at my ultrasound said, "It looks like we didn't get the whole thing."

My heart shattered. I was speechless and didn't know what to say. I was also confused. He explained that part of the fetus was still left inside of me and was causing an infection. The doctor said that they were going to have to do another surgery and the soonest appointment was the next day. I felt sick to my stomach. I ran out of the office and called my mom to tell her what was going on. This was by far one of the most traumatic things that has happened to me. There seemed to be bad things happening to me and it was getting to be too much for me to handle. It was bad enough to have one abortion, but to have two was too much for me emotionally and then to hear they didn't get the fetus all out of me was traumatic to say the least. On top of that, I had a scary infection and a fever. My mom was worried about me so she ended up taking off work and driving all the way from LA to San Clemente, which is a 3-hour drive. She didn't want me to be alone for this surgery. Dustin was out training, so he wouldn't be able to be there.

I went in the next day with my mom and did the procedure all over again. My mom then went back home and I was by myself through all of this and didn't really have anybody there to lean on. This is another event that I didn't like to tell many people because I'm ashamed and embarrassed. I just held it all in and drank away my feelings. I was depressed and it was not a good time for me in my life.

After having the abortion, it was really hard for me to want to stay with Dustin. Every time I looked at him, I was disgusted. It really screwed me up in the future with guys in general. I had an overall hatred for men. This was the second person that I had fallen in love and gotten pregnant with, and had them tell me they didn't want the baby. I don't want people to think other people made me get an abortion. Obviously it was my body and my choice, but at the end of the day, I was doing what I thought was best for me. Even though they were really hard and traumatic for me to deal with, they probably were for the best now looking back. There are days that I still regret those abortions and wonder what those kids would look like now. I miss them even though I never got to hold them. I will have to live with those abortions for the rest of my life. I'm only saying that now because I have a beautiful baby girl as I'm writing this. I think that if I didn't, I would regret it even more because I would think that those were my only chances to have kids. I also think my abortions, endometriosis, and severe case of gonorrhea made me infertile, so I did have to do IVF for my baby girl but that is for another book.

These are secrets I have held in for years and not something I'm proud of, but they are a part of my story. These times in my life made me grow up, learn from my mistakes, and made me who I am today. People who have abortions are not awful; everyone's situation is different. In my situation, I felt conflicted and that inner conflict has stayed with me since then. Either way, I was over my relationship with Dustin. I couldn't stay with someone who was so unsupportive and uncaring about what I wanted. I also didn't know how to properly process my feelings, so I would just get drunk every night and try to numb away my pain. Dustin had left for his last deployment and I was so alone. Alone, depressed, and drunk is never a good combination. I ended up cheating on Dustin that night. I don't like to call it cheating because in my mind we were already over, but technically we were still married. It was complicated. I don't know why I hooked up with a random person. I think it was my immature way of getting back at him for hurting me so deeply. I think I knew deep down because I loved him that if I didn't cheat on him and just tried to break up with him that there was a possibility of me getting back together with him. I knew it wouldn't be a healthy relationship so I had meaningless sex and cheated solely for that reason. I knew that would seal the deal for both of us. I called him the next day and told him what I had done, and like I imagined he broke up with me, called off the wedding, and we never spoke again. Actually, that is not true, months later we needed to get a divorce, which was crazy because we never in my eyes got "married" or had a wedding or anything. We went to court and as easily as we signed papers to get married, we signed papers to get a divorce and I gave him the ring back. It was super civil, neither of us owned anything, and we didn't have kids together so we signed the divorce papers, and we never spoke again.

CHAPTER 16

Back To Porn I Go

After divorcing Dustin, I decided that I was once again going to go back to porn because it was the one thing that I knew I liked and where I felt I belonged. At that point in my life, I was like fuck guys. I don't care about relationships anymore. I need to just focus on myself, make money, and put myself through school. I still wanted to get through nursing school because I knew I couldn't do porn forever. I wanted to have a back-up plan but I also wanted to do porn for a while because it was fun for me and I never got fired from porn. I also went back to escorting and I started traveling globally to escort with men and women all over the world.

My escorting agent would send me on these trips to New York so I would go for a week and I would see clients while I was out there and then travel back home because the demand for girls was really high in New York. How it works is you go out there and you get a really nice hotel that you stay in and then your clients either come to visit you at your hotel or you go out to them. I was seeing A LOT of clients in New York. Some of my clients would take me and a few other girls they hired to the Hamptons for a weekend. We would party with celebrities and models, we would take private jets all over, be wined and dined, and the best part was we were getting paid for it.

I met really wealthy people and one of them happened to be young and very good-looking. This also happened to be around the time I had REALLY low self-esteem. I didn't feel very good about myself with the people that I had fallen in love with in the past and I had given up on love. Every time I put myself all out on the line for someone, I was hurt so badly. I would uproot my life and move anywhere for them. I quit a job I loved that also paid well all because I was a hopeless romantic, but not anymore. I was JADED. I knew nobody wanted to have a kid with an ex-porn star and that no one would truly love me because of what I'd done. I would never have a real relationship. I was drinking a lot and I was unhappy. Even though I liked my job doing porn and escorting, I was still unhappy. I was not good at relationships, that was for sure. I ended up meeting a client and one of the biggest rules of escorting is to never date your clients. The rules are there for a reason, but you know me, I love to break the rules, so I decided that I was going to start dating one of my clients. This client lived in New York and he was a Wall Street guy. Guess what I ended up doing... I ended up moving to New York. Soho to be exact.

I lived above this store in SoHo

This was the street I lived on in SoHo New York

This guy was extremely controlling and did not treat me well at all, but I felt like no one could ever love me because I had done porn. I felt destroyed as a human. Mentally and physically, I was exhausted and the last thing I needed was to get into a relationship with this guy, but I needed to feel loved and even if it was just a little bit, I longed for it. I ended up in an abusive relationship with someone who treated me like shit and tried to control my life and everything that I did. We had gotten in a fight one night, a big one and there was a bar next door so I went to the bar and got super drunk. When I came back from the bar I walked into our house to find him completely naked having sex with another girl on our couch in the living room! I couldn't believe it.

When he got up and I was able to see the girl's face I realized it was a girl I knew. She was an escort who had also done porn. She recognized me and said, "Hey girl! What are you doing here?" I don't think she knew he was my boyfriend or that I lived there. I think she thought he also hired me for the night and we were going to have a threesome. I told the girl that he was my boyfriend. It was so awkward because she just said sorry but didn't know what to do. She wasn't leaving and he didn't ask her to leave so I ended up leaving because I didn't know how to deal with the situation. I went back to the bar and kept drinking. Drinking was the only way I knew how to numb my pain and deal with really fucked up situations. I feel like I should become a therapist for escorts and porn stars because no one in that line of work could confidently tell a therapist the fucked up shit we go through and not feel super judged or feel like they would call the cops on us for doing illegal shit. Anyway, I ended up getting too drunk and being carried by the bar owner back to my house because I passed out at the bar. I also ended up having alcohol poisoning and my boyfriend had to call an ambulance because he thought I was dead. I woke up when the paramedics got there and told them I was fine. The next day I booked a plane ticket home to LA. I was done with him. I remember walking out of his plush apartment building and it was snowing. I am a California girl and am not used to the snow. I was outside in the snow freezing my ass off. I was waiting for a taxi to take me to the airport and I couldn't wait to get out of there.

The strangeness of landing myself in that situation reminded me of one Halloween where I vividly remember going to a party I would never forget. It was by far the scariest Halloween I'd had. I was platinum blonde and I dressed in a sexy Little-Bo Peep costume that was super cute.

My Little Bo-Peep costume

I went to this party with my roommate at the time. This was a celebrity's party who I had recently started hooking up with and he was throwing a Halloween party. He was known to throw some amazing Halloween parties and told me to bring some of my girlfriends. I was so excited for this party and I knew a ton of other celebrities would be there so I went and got a spray tan, got my nails done, put extensions in and whitened my teeth. People at these parties went all out with their costumes so I wanted to make sure I wasn't going to be sticking out like a sore thumb at this party.

We pull up to his house in the hills and there are a ton of cars. It was a way bigger party than I thought it would be. He had valet outside to park everyone's car so we pulled up and gave the valet our car. I remember trying to walk up the hill to his house in my giant heels and was doing everything in my power not to fall. As we get closer to his house, celebrities are walking into this party with us. I started getting nervous because I was feeling a bit out of place. I didn't feel like I was good enough to be at this party because I did porn and all of the people there were important and famous and I was a nobody. If anyone knew who I was it was because maybe they jerked off to me. This is how I felt sober so I told my friend we need to find the alcohol ASAP.

Once I started drinking, I became more confident and fun and could hang out with celebrities and not be self-conscious. This house was decked out for Halloween. He had a team of professional decorators come out to decorate his house for the party and there was a live band playing fun Halloween party music. When you first walked in, they had it decorated to look like a haunted house, the entrance was lined with all these rad carved pumpkins all lit up as you walked in and there were cobwebs everywhere. The attention to detail was amazing. I love Halloween so I really appreciated the decor. There were so many people there and as I walked through the party in my search for the bar I got a dark Hollywood vibe from this party. I don't know how to describe it other than saying it was similar to what you felt when you watched the Hotel season of American Horror Story. It just felt like a very old Hollywood vibe that was a bit intimidating, but cool and also super creepy.

We finally found the bar in the backyard and I got myself a shot of vodka. He had a huge pool in his backyard and they had a bunch of dry ice in the pool so there was all this smoke coming out into the backyard. It looked all foggy and they had purple and orange lighting all over. They had a green light in the pool so it looked swampy and everything looked like it was straight out of a scary movie. The people that decorated his house probably worked for the movie sets and they did a killer job. I started drinking and getting more comfortable. I didn't really know any of the people at the party. I mean, I knew them because most of them were celebrities but we didn't personally know them and it is pretty intimidating to just walk up to someone super famous and be like, "Hi, I'm Channon, I do porn." Eventually, I saw the guy who was hosting the party, the guy I was hooking up with, and he came over to say hi to us and hung out with us for a bit but he was hosting a huge Halloween party so I didn't expect him to hang out with me the whole time.

He said he would meet back up with us later, but he was going to go say hi to some more people. He told us to have fun and we planned to. As the night went on, I was getting more drunk and I was still getting such a weird vibe from this party. An hour had passed and I had noticed that the guy I was hooking up with, let's call him Jerry, was holding this girl's hand and walking her downstairs to where his bedroom was. I knew that he was taking her there because the stairs that he was going down only went to his bedroom and his laundry room. I got jealous because I had been hooking up with him. I decided to drink even more because that is how I dealt with my feelings. I ended up getting so drunk that I decided I was going to go down to his room and see what was going on and if he was really hooking up with another girl at this party while I was there. I would NEVER, EVER do that sober, but I was drunk and thought that was MY MAN!

I walked downstairs and the door was unlocked so I opened it up and was shocked at what I saw. They were not having sex they were doing something way weirder than that. I've noticed that the more famous people are, the weirder they are. Actors are just weird people. This chick was on his bed and her shirt was half off and she had a big cut that was bleeding and he was licking the blood off of her. It took me a minute to figure out what was going on because it was Halloween so I didn't know if it was part of her costume or what. You never know what weird shit is going on at some of these parties, but this was by far something I hadn't seen before. It was like some Twilight shit going down. After a minute of my drunk ass staring at them, I realized this was not part of her Halloween costume and he was actually eating her blood off of her body. I thought at first I was drugged and tripping, but nope, this was actually happening. They looked at me and asked if I needed anything as if what they were doing was totally normal. I had just walked in on some weird shit. I didn't know what to say because I was so shocked and it wasn't like he was hooking up with her so I couldn't be mad at him. So I said I came down to say hi and then I shut the door and walked back upstairs because I didn't know what else to do.

Ten minutes later he came up to me at the party and asked if I was okay. I looked at him and said, "Do you mean, are YOU okay? I am sure I just saw you eating some chick's blood you weirdo vampire!" He smiled at me and replied with, "Happy Halloween" in a creepy voice. I looked at him like I am not drunk enough for this. Thirty minutes later, I started to feel really weird. I felt like I had been drugged. I think that Jerry drugged me but I wasn't positive. I just don't know who else would have drugged me. The rest of the night I was tripping out. The whole night was fuzzy and all I remember is Jerry taking all these different girls down to his room. I thought he was hooking up with all these random girls throughout the night. Every time someone walked by me I would hear these people whispering in my ear, "Are you thirsty?" Whatever drugs he gave me almost felt like an acid trip and I felt like I was in a house full of vampires on Halloween night that were getting away with drinking girls' blood. I thought they were all trying to turn me into a vampire by the end of the night. It was SO scary! I felt so helpless.

I kept telling my friend that everyone there was a vampire and that they were all drinking blood and they were going to try and turn me into a vampire and that we needed to leave. My poor friend was probably thinking, damn girl what drugs are you on? I just wanted to leave the party. As I was walking around, I started to feel really horny, so I'm not sure if he gave me a mix of acid and ecstasy or if the ecstasy was laced.

I didn't know, but as we were getting ready to leave, Jerry came over to me and grabbed my hand. He started kissing my neck and whispered in my ear to come downstairs with him. Between his hotness and whatever drugs I was on, I couldn't resist so I went downstairs with him. We walked into his bedroom and I thought we were going to have sex and he is going to turn me into a vampire and I am too horny to stop this. My fate had been chosen for me. He was seducing me and he was in to some weird shit. As he started undressing me he pulled out a knife and cut me and started licking my blood. I was so fucked up on drugs by this time that I just went with it and I was so horny I didn't care. I did ask him though why he was cutting me in this specific spot near my ribs because it was a weird spot to cut someone in. He explained to me that it is a spot that will always be hidden. No matter what you wear, your bra strap, tank top, or tee shirt will always cover it. He had this well thought out and planned. I wondered how many times he had done this, but I didn't care that he was doing it. He ate my blood and then had sex with me. I didn't know if he had sex with all the girls he brought down to his room, but the drugs I was on made me not even care. I still to this day think this celebrity is a vampire. I used to not believe in witches and vampires, but they exist and that is all I'm going to say. I believe that they exist because I have experienced them in person. You can think I am making it up or call me crazy, but why do you think witches, werewolves, and vampires are always consistent in books and movies? It is because they are REAL.

CHAPTER 17

Dating My Clients

The client in New York was the first client I dated. The second one was probably my most high-profile client ever. He was the heir of a very well-known bank and investment company. I didn't meet him through my agency but through a friend who also saw him. She told me I would meet him at a hotel and wouldn't tell me who he was. When I met up with him, I was pleasantly surprised because he was good-looking, and he was really cool and fun. I spent the night with him in his hotel and after that night, he wanted to date me. I finally found out who he was after we started dating because he didn't want to tell me for obvious reasons. I just knew he had a lot of money and maybe did something important, but I had no clue what it was. Once I found out, I had been so used to being around high-profile celebrities and public figures that it really wasn't that big of a deal to me. I didn't know at the time but he had a serious drug problem. I noticed occasionally he would doze off, but I didn't do drugs during this time, I only drank a lot, so I would get really drunk and not know exactly what he was doing. He definitely hid that he was doing drugs and I don't know the exact drugs he was doing, but I'm pretty sure he was doing heroin and probably taking a ton of Xanax and mixing that with wine. I'm really lucky that he never ended up dying on me. We will call him Mr. M.

Mr. M had a place in an undisclosed location and I got to stay there all the time. I felt so fancy when we hung out. Everywhere we went people catered to us as if we were royalty. Well, he kind of was, but I was far from it. He flew me back and forth from LA to his house and he didn't care that I did porn, he just didn't want me escorting with other people. One thing about Mr. M was he was really weird with his money. He would always ask if I was dating him for his money and I would always have to reassure him that I was actually losing money by dating him because he didn't want me to escort.

What I'm saying is I didn't need his money. I wasn't with him for the money. I wasn't a gold digger and wasn't trying to marry this guy. I am sure he has had to deal with all kinds of weird people because of who he was, but he didn't have to worry about me. Deep down, I think he knew that. We would go on so many fun trips but he was on drugs the whole time and I didn't know that. The fact that he was on drugs didn't dawn on me until I ended up in Mexico with him and one of my girlfriends I invited.

On our trip in Mexico

Living my best life in Mexico

He had a huge house in Mexico on the water and our trip was going great. We were out one night clubbing in Mexico living our best life, and then I started looking around for Mr. M and he was nowhere to be found. I started getting worried because we were in the middle of Mexico at a club, just me and my girlfriend and I didn't even know how to get back to the house we were staying at. I was convinced someone was holding him hostage for ransom or something crazy. We went looking everywhere trying to find him. Neither of us had brought money with us to the club, so we couldn't even try to get to a hotel. I tried calling him a million times, but his phone was off. We were stuck in Mexico and my boyfriend had disappeared. We somehow managed to get a ride and find the house we were staying in but Mr. M was not there. The next day came around and he was still missing. I was a wreck. I didn't know what to do. We called the hospitals, the police, but no one knew where he was. I was really worried and concerned because we were in a different country. It was a really fucked up situation. We felt like we were stranded. We finally made it safely back home to find that Mr. M had left Mexico entirely and was at his house safe and sound.

We ended up finding out that he went to try and get drugs when we were out at the club but he couldn't find any. He must have ran out of all of his drugs and so he booked it back home to the States and full-on left my friend and I behind in Mexico. Not cool. I guess that is what drugs do to you. I remember when we were in Mexico, we were searching all around the house looking for him and I went into the bathroom, and I saw a bunch of pill bottles with the labels all ripped off. He wanted to make sure his name and information were not left behind. That is when I realized, "Oh fuck, my boyfriend is probably a drug addict." He ran out of pills and left me in Mexico. I later found out after that whole situation that his assistant put him in rehab and I didn't talk to him again after that.

After Mr. M, I dated Dustin Flynt who is the nephew of Larry Flynt of Hustler. They all work in the family business and I ended up meeting Dustin and we started dating. That relationship was a bit different because he was such a Playboy. We had an open relationship, so it was okay for him to hook up with other girls and me to hook up with other guys but we were still together and dating each other. We would have crazy sex parties, he would get me to invite all my friends over, and we would all get drunk and do drugs. He was fun to date because he understood the adult entertainment world.

However, I soon found out I was dating somebody I didn't know very much about. He decided to fly me in his private jet to Oklahoma to his hometown because he thought it would be fun for me to go experience it. One of the days we were there, he told me he needed to run an errand real quick. I told him it was no problem. We drove over to this really nice house and parked right in front. He smiled at me and kissed me before he got out of the car and said, "Be right back." I then watched this girl come out of the house holding a baby. I thought to myself, how sweet he's stopping by to visit his sister and her baby.

When he got back in the car I said what a cute baby, who's baby is that? He nonchalantly said, "Oh that's mine and she is my wife." I was just like, "What the fuck? Are you kidding me? You are just now telling me that you are married?! And have a kid!!!???" He just brushed it off like it was no big deal. He told me he thought because I did porn that I wouldn't care. Just because I did porn didn't mean I had no morals whatsoever. I didn't have many, but I had some. That was just crossing the line for me. I guess the wife knew that he did stuff like this, but I didn't and I just didn't feel comfortable doing that. In the back of my mind, I always pictured myself getting married one day and having kids and it just didn't feel right. It is different when I'm working but I was dating him so to me it was different. I had fun with our sex parties and open relationship but what I really wanted was a monogamous relationship. When I found out he was married with a kid that ended our relationship pretty quickly.

CHAPTER 18

I'm An Idiot

I was still doing porn and one of my ex-boyfriends, Joe, the one from the beginning of the book, had gotten a hold of me. I was still not in a good place in life. I was in and out of bad relationships and had shitty self-esteem. I was broken. Joe still didn't have a job and was most likely calling to use me for a place to live or money, who knows. I of course didn't see it like that at the time because I wanted to pretend like he still loved me, but he didn't. He just wanted to use me for a place to live and money. I was in a nice new apartment and living alone, and I hated living alone and had just broken up with Dustin Flynt, so like a sucker, I let Joe move in with me rent-free. He had his own room in the house and I even bought his weed for him because I was a SUCKER and STUPID. A few weeks later, I ran into an old friend from elementary school. She was in a rough spot, didn't have a job, and needed a place to stay. I of course wanted to help her out and I was in a position to do so, so I did. I let her move in until she was able to get on her own two feet. I had two people living with me who didn't have jobs and were total stoners. They both smoked weed together and never even tried to look for jobs. I was supporting them, buying their food, even buying their weed, and providing a place for them to live for free. I know this sounds really bad but I think a part of me felt like I needed to pay people to hang out with me. I ended up hooking up with Joe because he was living with me and it was convenient. I would say we were kind of dating. We didn't always sleep in the same bed every night, but we would hook up because I was lonely. Then one thing led to another and he convinced me to only do girl-on-girl porn because he would get jealous if I was sleeping with other guys.

A few months passed, then I ended up having to travel for work. I let Joe use my truck while I was out of town and asked him to pick me up when I got back to LA. I waited at the airport for awhile waiting for him to pick me up. I kept calling him but he wasn't answering his phone. I started getting worried thinking something happened to him. I ended up calling one of our mutual friends to see if she knew where he was because I knew he was at her house last. When I called her, I had asked if she knew where he was and she said no, but that she needed to tell me something. Whatever it was it didn't sound good, so I braced myself for some bad news. She told me Joe had been cheating on me with the friend living with me, the one I'd known since elementary school. My heart dropped into my stomach and I felt like I couldn't breathe. I asked her how long it had been going on and she said it started two weeks after she moved in. I felt like I was going to throw up. She then told me that all three of them had a threesome the night before last at her house. I had never felt so betrayed by so many people that were so close to me in my life. I had been helping both of them when they needed it the most, how could they do something like this to me? I had to get a taxi home from the airport because they had my car. I cried the whole way home. Still to this day, I don't let friends get too close to me in fear of getting hurt again. It had happened to me too many times before and this was the last straw for me. I kicked them both out and never talked to them again.

CHAPTER 19

Escaping The Mental Ward With My Bestie

After all that shit went down with Joe and my so-called friends, I decided I needed to stop dating altogether. I felt like I couldn't trust anyone but at the same time I needed an assistant for work that I could trust. There was a woman who was always bugging me to let her work as my assistant so I hired her. I needed an assistant because my life and my schedule was all over the place and I was always busy. She was cool, she wasn't weird about the porn industry, and was chill and down to party with me, so we were a good match. We'll call her Mallory. I ended up getting a new apartment because I had too many bad memories from the old one. I also got bored easily and wanted to move for a fresh start.

When I hired Mallory, instead of being paid, she wanted to live with me for free, and I would just pay for everything for her. Her living with me worked out well in my favor because a live-in assistant is GOLD in LA. I paid for all her food, clothes, alcohol when we went out, and basically whatever she wanted. She was previously living at her parents' house, had no job, and wanted to live the Hollywood lifestyle so she got exactly that living with me. If I bought something for myself, I would buy double for her. If I was buying makeup, I bought her makeup, if I was buying a dog, I bought her dog. I felt like she was paid to be my best friend and help me out with my schedule. It sounds horrible but it's just the truth.

She started to do everything with me and we became best friends. She hung out with me everywhere I went, came to set with me, came to my appearance's, AVN, basically EVERYWHERE. I was a drunk mess so it was her job to try to keep me on track and on schedule, although the majority of the time we just partied a lot. When we weren't working we would go to clubs in Hollywood every night. We would sleep until 3 or 4 in the afternoon, eat Taco Bell, smoke cigarettes, get drunk before leaving for the club, drink more on the way to the club, and then we would drink even more once we got there. We were always drunk. Mallory also did cocaine, but she was more secretive about it; first of all because it was illegal, second because she was supposed to be keeping me in line and not the other way around, and third because I didn't do drugs other than drink most of the time, so she probably felt weird doing it around me.

I'm sure she did other drugs but I only saw her do cocaine. Some nights she would get more fucked up than I would. She started making friends in Hollywood and a lot of people in the mainstream entertainment industry. I wouldn't call her a social climber but she was good at making friends with important people. If you weren't important, she wouldn't want to have anything to do with you. But she was cool and fun to hang out with and we were best friends. One night we were out at a club in LA and we were doing what we did every night. This night there happened to be a celebrity there. Mallory went up to him to talk to him and he asked who I was. She told him I was a porn star. I guess he wanted to talk to me or hook up with me but I didn't even know he was there. She never said anything to me about it. The next day we were at home watching a movie and I told Mallory how I had the biggest crush on this guy in the movie. She laughed and said he was at the club last night asking about you. I told her to shut up, because I didn't believe her. She told me she was trying to hit on him and he was just asking about me. I was like, "Oh my God, I can't believe that you didn't say something I'm like obsessed with this guy!" I thought he was so hot and she said, "I have his number."

We ended up meeting him at the same club the next night. We got really drunk at the club and headed back to his place. We were trying to have a threesome with him, but he didn't want to hook up with Mallory. That was okay for me, because I had the biggest crush on this guy and we actually ended up dating. Then at the same time, Mallory started dating this guy who was a rock star and we'd all go out together. Our lives were crazy. Anytime paparazzi saw me with my actor boyfriend, we had to pretend we didn't know each other. We couldn't walk into the club together; we had to go separately. We'd even have to drive to places separately. We couldn't eat out together at restaurants. It would ruin his career to be seen with me. It was fucked up because I had to hide my relationship. I had a secret relationship with a celebrity. It was horrible. He had to leave to film a show in Canada and was going to be gone for a while but we still talked. It was kind of an on and off relationship.

During this time, I got booked for the Howard Stern Show, which is in New York. Mallory and I flew to New York to do the Howard Stern Show and I did some escorting while I was there. I was a full-blown alcoholic at this time and was constantly drinking. As soon as we got to NYC, we decided to hit the bars. We were up all night drinking and I had the Howard Stern Show super early in the morning, like 5 am which is 2 am California time. Not only was I super tired, but I was also pretty nervous because I grew up watching Howard

THE STORY OF CHANNON ROSE

Stern and he was known to be brutally honest and often mean. I was scared he was going to tear me apart. I kept second-guessing if I wanted to go on the show because I didn't know if it was worth it, but I did have a porn website at the time and I thought it would be good exposure, so I put my big girl panties on and went for it.

I went in expecting the worst. I was expecting him to tell me I was not the most attractive and that my body could use some work in the gym. We went through security and they put my assistant and I in the green room. Once inside the green room we could hear them on the radio. It was finally time for me to go on the radio. I looked so busted up because I did my makeup quickly and I wasn't that great at makeup at the time. I was so nervous walking into his radio show. As I walked in, everyone on the show was SO nice to me. Howard said that I was too good-looking to do porn, whatever that meant. I was shocked. I was ready to get ripped to pieces, but he told me I was pretty! I couldn't believe it. While I was on the show, they asked me a bunch of porn questions. Then, because they knew I had gone to nursing school they played a game with me where they put me in a tickle chair, strapped me down and asked me a bunch of nursing questions. Each time I got them right they would plug my website, if I got them wrong they would tickle me. I got most of the questions right. I am really glad that I had the opportunity to go on the show and it was a really cool experience for me.

After the show you would think I would be on cloud nine. My interview went WAY better than I had expected, my website traffic shot through the roof and I was making a lot more money from the site and Howard promoting it. But, for some reason, I had this overwhelming sadness inside of me. I hated feeling that way especially when I felt like I was supposed to be happy. I only knew one way to cure that and that was with vodka. Mallory and I decided to start drinking again that night so we hit the bars and got super drunk. Getting drunk was my way of self-medicating. Most of the times when I drank I was happy, fun, and confident, but then there were times when I drank that I would get even more depressed than I already was and it was a recipe for disaster. Sometimes when I drank, something would happen in my head and my mind would flood with all the horrible memories I had in my life. You know how sometimes in movies they portray flashbacks of someone's life before they die? It's almost as if they see their life playing like a movie before their eyes. When I would get super depressed and I was drunk, I would see my life flash before my eyes like a movie playing, but I could only see the horrible bad memories of my life. It was awful. I would try to drink more to try to get rid of the memories but it would never work.

I started cutting myself because it would distract me from the bad memories and feelings. Each time I would cut my wrist the emotional pain I was feeling would fade to physical pain and even though the physical pain was only temporary, it was so refreshing and felt so good to have a break in my mind without those awful emotional feelings. Sometimes that wasn't enough though and I knew that break wasn't going to last and my pain was too great of a burden to bear. I would pray for the strength to cut deeper and slowly just fade away. I would fantasize in these moments that I would cut myself deep enough to slowly bleed to death. I would picture myself drunk enough that I wasn't scared and that I would just slowly fall asleep and feel no more pain. It would feel amazing and so freeing for the first time in my life to feel no pain or hurt. I was in so much pain that I became suicidal. I wanted to end my pathetic life. The pain I kept feeling over and over wouldn't go away no matter how much I drank or how much I mutilated my body. It was too much for me to handle. I couldn't go on any longer. I would also like to point out that if you knew me during that time in my life you would have NEVER known that I was suicidal or suffered from suicidal ideations. On the outside, I seemed happy. I was always having fun and the life of the party. Only the people closest to me knew what was really going on in my mind.

That is an especially scary aspect of people who struggle with their mental health. Some people can be really good at hiding it. I know I was. These people can show absolutely no signs at all that they have anything wrong with them. For me, most people had no idea. That is why I always try to be nice to people, we never know what people are going through on the inside. We can't always see what people are actually feeling. Sometimes it is the last person you would think to be suicidal who ends up taking their life because the pain is too much to bear. For some reason, people think that people who are famous, or have a lot of money, or a great job, or even a great relationship or marriage can't be depressed because they have a "good life." This is simply not the case. It doesn't matter who you are or what you have or don't have, ANYONE can be affected by this disease. I have heard statements suggesting that people who end their lives are cowards or are selfish to leave behind their kids or families and it makes me sick. I can't stand hearing people speak so terribly of someone with a mental disorder. You are not in that person's shoes. You cannot even imagine how much pain someone has to be in to make that decision. Let me say it like this, imagine being in the worst pain of your life, like someone is stabbing you over and over again. Now imagine knowing that pain will never go away. Every day from the moment you wake up until the moment you go to bed, you are in agony and unable to concentrate, focus, or even enjoy anything. You are suffering and nothing is making it go away. Now imagine dealing with that for weeks, months, or maybe even years. That is just a taste of what depression feels like.

NO one wants to commit suicide. These people are in so much pain that they can't bear the thought of living another day. Do you know how awful that feels? So be nice to people. You never know what they are going through. Even those without mental illnesses are dealing with other problems and issues in life. No one's life is perfect so let's be nicer to each other. It is important to remember that help for depression exists, and it is possible to get better. If you are feeling anything similar to how I was feeling that night, I encourage you to speak to someone, anyone, about it.

Anyways, I got back to my hotel room that night and I was having a bad night. I was getting the movie flashback of all my awful memories in my life and even though I was drinking more, the bad thoughts wouldn't go away. I think from the outside looking in, I had this really cool lifestyle. Doing porn wasn't socially acceptable, but it was fun and I was making a ton of money. I was able to travel the world, I was hanging out with celebrities and able to buy whatever I wanted. But I was still so unhappy and depressed and all I wanted to do was kill myself. When I got back to my hotel, I got my razor blade out of my suitcase, grabbed my bottle of vodka and a cigarette, went into the hotel bathroom, and shut the door. I told Mallory I wanted to be left alone for awhile. I put on some sad music and got naked. I got into the bathtub and lit my cigarette, drank the rest of the bottle of vodka and started to cut my wrists. I cried. All I wanted was to be happy. I didn't care about money or fame or having a cool life. It wasn't what I really wanted. I'd rather be broke and happy, but that wasn't my reality so I kept cutting my wrists. My plan was to cut myself deep enough so I would bleed to death and I could fall asleep drunk in the bathtub and just never wake up.

I cut myself so much that there was blood EVERYWHERE. I called my boyfriend at the time and told him I loved him and goodbye. He knew I had issues and that I was in trouble so he called the NYC police and they called the fire department to do a wellness check on me. I still don't know how they figured out which hotel or room number I was in because I never even told my boyfriend where I was staying. Somehow I ended up from the bathtub wanting to kill myself, to doing cartwheels naked covered in blood down the hotel hallway with Mallory. That is how my brain worked; call it bipolar disorder or what you will, but my mood changed so much that I was happy again and having fun. Maybe that is how they found me because other guests may have called the cops on us. Mallory had also cut her wrists and before we knew it, we were both in the back of an ambulance heading to a state psychiatric hospital. They normally don't transport two people in one ambulance but somehow we were both in the back and we kept trying to make out with each other and they had to keep separating us. One minute I was trying to kill myself, the next minute I was doing cartwheels, and then I was restrained in the back of an ambulance making out with my best friend. I was a nutcase! I still am, but a much more toned down version. That is one of the many reasons I don't drink anymore.

Hours later I remember waking up in this state psychiatric hospital in New York city, Bellevue Hospital. I went to get up but I couldn't, I was restrained to the bed. I panicked. I was still a little drunk but I was sober enough to think to myself, what the fuck have I gotten myself into? I couldn't remember much or how I had gotten there. I started calling for a nurse because I wanted to let them know that my flight home was only a few hours away and to see if they could speed up the process of getting me out of there. It was a long shot since most psych hospitals have a policy of keeping patients who are a danger to themselves or others for at least 72 hours. Moments later, someone walked into my room but it wasn't a nurse, it was Mallory! I was so excited to see her but also confused. How did they just let her in my room like that? I asked her how she got in my room, she replied, "I was brought in with you, you idiot!" I looked down at her arms and realized she had bandages covering one of her arms. Then it made more sense to me. I asked, "How did you get out of your restraints?" She said, "I was never put in any. You were acting like a wild hyena when we came in here so that is why you look like this." I told her stop making jokes and to undo my restraints. She laughed and as she was unbuckling my restraints she went into work mode and told me she needed to get us out of there so we didn't miss our flight. It was one of the reasons I loved her so much. Even when we were both locked up in a mental ward she was thinking about getting me back to LA for my next job.

We realized once I was out of my restraints that we were going to have to figure out how to escape the psych ward, which wouldn't be easy because we both looked like we belonged there. Our hair and makeup was a hot mess and we wreaked of vodka and cigarettes. We both had bandages on our arms from our wrists to our elbows and we were in hospital gowns with those awful anti-slip grip hospital socks on. We looked at each other and couldn't help but laugh because as always our lives were like a movie and no one would ever believe half of the stuff that happened to us. We got lucky because the nurses were on their shift change so they were all in one area, and we somehow managed to get out! One of us may or may not have sucked some dick to escape. When we left the hospital, we were still in our hospital gowns and anti-slip socks. We didn't know how we were going to get back to our hotel because it wasn't walking distance. We ended up flagging down a taxi and figured we would get money from our room and bring it back down to the cab driver once he dropped us off. By some miracle, Mallory found a $20 dollar bill on the floor of the taxi, which covered the fare. We were then able to run in to our hotel, pack our shit, and head to the airport to catch our flight home. Believe it or not, we actually made our original flight home, which was nothing short of a miracle.

CHAPTER 20

I Bought A Haunted House

I decided I wanted to buy my first house because I wanted to finally finish nursing school and I had saved enough money for a down payment. I figured I could stop doing porn for a bit while I went to school and I could rent out the other rooms in the house to other college students to help pay the mortgage.

The first house I bought that was SUPER haunted

That way I wouldn't have to work and could go to school full-time. I was so excited that I could buy my own house, especially at such a young age. I ended up buying a 3-bedroom house in LA with a guesthouse in the back. I rented out all the rooms in the main house and I lived in the back guesthouse, but I was having a really hard time keeping roommates. They kept moving out and I didn't understand

THE STORY OF CHANNON ROSE

why because it was a cool place to live and it was close to campus. One by one, a new roommate would move in and then shortly after move out. There was a time when there were all girls living at my house and it was so fun. It felt like a little sorority house. I became friends with the girls quickly and I remember one night going into the main house and one of the girls telling me that my prank call earlier that day was really funny. I looked at her confused because I never prank called her. I hadn't known her that long, but I wasn't the pranking type. I told her it must have been someone else. Then the other roommate said she got a prank phone call too from someone who said it came from me. The girls didn't believe me because the caller ID said it came from my phone. As I was sitting there trying to convince them that I didn't call them, one of the girls got a call. She picked up her phone and showed me that it was coming from my phone.

I went over to my phone and it wasn't calling anyone. We all freaked out. I told her to answer it. She answered it and put it on speaker so we could all hear. A voice came from the phone and it was the spookiest voice I had ever heard. He said he was going to kill all of us. I grabbed the phone and hung up on whoever it was. My heart was pounding. The house was not gated, none of us had guns, and we were so scared. I didn't know how they got our numbers or how they were able to call them and it show that it was coming from my phone. We ended up calling the cops, but the cops never showed up. I think they didn't believe us. We ended up going to the police station and hanging out there for a while that night because we were all too scared to be at the house and felt safer at the police station. We eventually had to go back home that night and we all slept in the main house together because I was too scared to sleep in the guesthouse alone.

That was the first really scary experience I had in the house, but not once did I think it was the actual house itself. I just thought it was a crazy stalker from my porn days or someone trying to scare us.

One of the girls that lived in the house was a very spiritual girl. She was going to school for an alternative medicine called Reiki. She had a spirit board that she wanted me to use with her and I always said no because it honestly kind of scared me. It looked like a Ouija board but she always said that it was to contact only good spirits and that it would be fun. During that time, all of us girls had become closer and we were hanging out more. Also, during this time neither one of the girls said anything to me about anything weird going on in the house. One night we were all drinking in the main house and the spiritual roommate said, "Let's all use the spirit board!" She was so excited and always wanting to use the board with us. She said that she had spirit guides and they would help guide her through life and we could contact our spirit guides through the board. I was drunk so I said I would finally do it with her. She went into her room to get the board ready for us to play, and when she was done she told us to come into her room. When I walked in, her room was pitch black with about 100 candles lit around the board. It looked like a séance was about to go down. I told her she better not burn my house down with the million candles lit in her room.

We were all joking around and giving her a hard time because we were drunk and it was fun and easy to make fun of her. She knew we loved her though. She explained to us the 'rules' of the board and made us all say a prayer to protect us while we were using the spirit board. That should have been my sign to run out of that room but my drunk ass just went along with it. She asked me to ask the board a question.

I went ahead and thought of a question that I knew for sure these girls wouldn't know the answer to. I asked the board the date of my bad car accident when I almost died. The board started moving and said the exact date that I was in my car accident! I instantly freaked out. I didn't even believe this board was real! I started crying and the roommate that knew about the board comforted me. She told me it was my spirit guide that was communicating with me and that it was a good thing and to not be scared but to keep communicating through the board with them. She told me to ask the spirit another question. I had always thought that my grandma on my mom's side who had passed away when I was younger was my guardian angel. We called her Mommy Dee. I asked the board if anyone was there with me when my accident happened. I always thought maybe Mommy Dee was there protecting me and watching over me when I was in my accident because I should have died that day. I was airlifted to UCLA hospital, paralyzed from the waist down and the doctors didn't think I would make it. The board then started spelling out Mommy Dee! I went into shock and disbelief. I didn't know how to react other than to cry and laugh but then I got scared by all of this. How was this happening? I ended up leaving the room because I was scared of whatever was going on. I didn't know how to process everything and I was drunk so I was done playing with the board. My roommate said I needed to close out a prayer before I finished but I was too scared to go back in her room so I left. My two roommates did a closing out prayer and that was that.

Two weeks had gone by when the spiritual roommate went into her room and came out asking me if I took her spirit board out of the trash and put it on her bed. I told her no. She looked at the other roommate and she also said no. I then stopped and said, "Wait, why did you throw your board away?" She told us she didn't want us to get mad at her so she didn't want to say anything but that when she used it last something evil came through and it scared her so she threw it away. I was like OH HELL NAH GIRL! And now she was telling us that it magically appeared back on her bed on it's own!? I knew that board was bad news. She called her mom to ask for advice because apparently the girl's mom is also into this stuff. The mom told us that we couldn't throw the board away because whatever was going on would get worse. We were instructed to leave the board in the garage and to not mess with it. We all agreed and left the board alone in the garage.

Two months after that incident happened, the girl ended up moving out. But here is the kicker… she left her board in my garage! Shortly after, my other roommate moved out. Neither one of them said why they were moving but at this point I was so used to roommates moving in and out that I was over it. I personally encountered something really scary one day in broad daylight when I walked out of my guesthouse and noticed a young guy in the backyard. I had never seen him before but I had three roommates and they always had friends over, so I assumed it was one of my roommates' friends. I said hi to him but he never said anything back to me so I just kept walking to my car to go get food. When I came back to the house, he was gone. I thought he was weird but didn't think anything about it afterwards. A few days later I was in the main house with my roommates and I had asked whose friend was in the backyard because he seemed weird and when I said hi, he ignored me. All my roommates said they didn't have any friends over the past few days so I thought that was really strange. I was then wondering who the hell was in our backyard. I got a bad feeling about it and felt that something wasn't right about that person. It turned out that I was right, but I didn't find out why until years later. It ended up being one of the most terrifying events in my life, I just didn't know it at the time.

I once again had new roommates move in and one of them came up to me one day and told me that some weird things were happening to him at night in the house. I asked him what they were and he said that he thought there was a succubus visiting him at night. At first I thought maybe he could possibly be making it up, but then I realized that he seemed pretty stable and was actually quite scared of whatever was going on at night in the house. He said he didn't say anything at first because he didn't want us to think he was weird. I told him I believed him but to not say anything to the other roommates because I didn't want them to be scared off by this guy or my house. I had a hard enough time keeping roommates and it was a pain to keep having new people moving in all the time. A few days later another roommate came up and asked me if anyone had ever experienced anything in my house that was ever out of the ordinary. I asked her, "Why?" She said she had been experiencing some weird things in the house. I really didn't want her to move out because I wouldn't be able to pay the whole mortgage on my own. I wasn't working during that time and I also didn't want to be left alone in the house, so I dismissed it. A week or so had passed and I had walked into the main house and all three of the roommates living there were all sitting on the couch talking about how the house was haunted. I didn't want to believe it. They told me that we needed to get a paranormal team out to come and investigate the house but at the time I tried to brush it off and not deal with it.

I did have things occur in my guest house as well but I just wrote them off and thought to myself that there had to be a logical explanation for them. I did from time to time always feel like someone was in the room with me and then when I would turn around there would be no one there. I also always had the feeling someone was in the bathroom when I was taking a shower and I would move the shower curtain to see who it was but no one was in the bathroom. Sometimes I would see someone in the corner of my eye but no one was there. This would happen to me from time to time, but I just thought it was normal. My roommates that were living there finally convinced me to get a paranormal team to come investigate. It would be free, so I agreed. Now I was scared because everything was starting to add up. It made sense to me why all my roommates kept moving out. I figured they must not have said anything because they didn't want me to think they were crazy or maybe they were too scared to talk about it. The paranormal team that showed up came from a college that studied the scientific aspect of paranormal phenomena and when they showed up, 22 people came out to investigate my house.

I was shocked as I thought maybe only two people were coming. We left the house and they set up all these cameras and devices all over the house and were there for hours. They told us after that night that there is definitely paranormal activity and that they needed time to go over all the footage and review it and then they would give us an overview if they found anything. After their review, they informed me that the house behind us that was abandoned had a tragic story to it. They said there was a kid who lived there who killed his whole family in the house, then called the police and locked himself inside. The SWAT team came out and was trying to get this kid out, but the kid ended up shooting two SWAT officers, killing one of them. The house caught on fire, the kid came out shooting, and the SWAT team shot and killed him. They also explained that ghosts or spirits can move house to house and that is likely what had happened when we used the spirit board. They had printed out pictures of the tragedy to show me what happened, and when they showed me a picture of the kid that killed his family in that house, it was THE SAME PERSON THAT I TALKED TO IN MY BACKYARD years earlier who ignored me. I talked to a ghost!

The woman in charge of the investigation was too scared to come back to my house because whatever was in the house had personally attacked her that night and it scared her to the point that she wouldn't come back. When they sat down with us, they told us that out of the 5 years they've been investigating, our house had the most activity they had ever seen. I owned this house so I still had to live in it until I was able to sell it. I was definitely going to be selling this house because I was way too scared to keep living there. My mom also personally had experienced stuff that happened to her at my house when she would visit. When she went to the bathroom, someone whispered in her ear and she also saw things fall off counters and shelves while she was there. I remember later on when we were selling the house (we sold it ourselves, not with a realtor for obvious reasons), my mom would sit outside on a chair in the driveway because she was too scared to go back inside my house. When people came to look at the house she would tell them to feel free to check it out but she wouldn't go in the house herself.

My dad is a total biker dude, buff, and a huge skeptic when it comes to ghosts. My dad had stayed in my guesthouse one night and he woke up in the middle of the night hearing tapping noises on the windows and then he started hearing them on the roof. He didn't know what they were so he just figured we were messing with him so he fell back asleep. The next morning he came into the main house and said we were funny trying to mess with him last night. We looked at him funny because we had actually fallen asleep early that night and we never messed with him. We wrote it off, but a few days later something really creepy and scary happened. It was late at night and my dad had just fallen asleep, it was around 1 or 2 am and my dad said that he started feeling a weird tingling feeling that started from his head and went all the way down through his body into his toes. He explained it as this ghost that went in and through his body and he recounts that when the ghost was in his body he thought he was dead until it left his body. He was definitely convinced after that incident that my house was haunted.

Another crazy thing that happened was one night my boyfriend and I were planning on watching a movie in the main house and I had this wall of crosses that I had collected from all over the world. All the crosses on the wall had at least 3 nails each keeping them secure because we live in California and have earthquakes. I didn't want them to break because some of them were ceramic. We also had lots of parties so needless to say they were secure on the wall. I was taking a shower before we started our movie and my boyfriend was on the couch watching TV. While I was in the shower, he heard someone knocking on the door so he opened the front door and no one was there. When he shut the door, he heard a loud bang at the back of the house and as he was walking to the back of the house he walked through the hallway with all the crosses on the wall and as he was walking by he heard a scraping noise on the wall. When he looked over he watched one of the crosses turn on its own and flip upside down. He didn't want to scare me so he didn't tell me what happened. After I got out of the shower someone was knocking on the door again, so he went to answer it, and again, no one was there. We just ignored it and started watching our movie.

About thirty minutes in to our movie we hear a huge bang coming from the back of the house. I asked my boyfriend to go in the backyard to see if he could see what was making the noise. He went back there but he couldn't find where the noise was coming from so we just figured it was the water heater. We went back to watching the movie and as the movie was about to end, we heard the noise again but this time it was even louder. I asked him to check one more time to see if he could see what the noise was. He was hesitant and just said it was nothing and I started getting mad at him because I wanted to know what the noise was. He finally agreed but told me he wanted me to come with him. I said I was scared and wanted to stay in the house and he told me no. We argued back and forth and he finally just said he didn't want me in the house alone. We went in the backyard with a flashlight and looked around to see where the noise was coming from. We didn't see anything in the backyard so we went back inside the house. I went to the bathroom and as I walked over to the bathroom I looked over to the wall that had all the crosses on it and every last one of them was flipped upside down! I screamed, pissed my pants, and ran out of the house. My boyfriend came running after me and I told him we were staying in a hotel. We stayed in a hotel for a week. I ended up renting the house out and getting my own apartment because I was too scared to go back after that night. We ended up having a family friend go and take all the crosses off the wall before we rented it out. There was more than just a ghost in that house; there was something demonic in there.

CHAPTER 21

A Whole New World

After being in porn for so many years, I noticed that things in the adult industry started to change and not in a good way. It all started when people started posting free porn online. After that, websites started popping up that were dedicated to sharing free porn. Thanks Pornhub. They would post free porn but these sites would get paid because they had ads on the videos. That really hurt our industry. The same thing was happening to the music industry and it was all happening at the same time. I started getting booked less jobs, and people were wanting to pay lower rates because the porn companies weren't making as much money as they used to, so they weren't able to book and pay us as much as they were before. Then porn started becoming a bit more mainstream so more girls wanted to do porn. Our industry soon became oversaturated with girls coming into the industry. These new girls were only charging $500 per scene instead of the $1,200 rate we normally would charge. Instead of these girls signing with an agency, they had managers who would take a percentage of their check and it was turning into a mess. The managers were taking advantage of these new girls by taking upwards of 30% of their earnings, which is absurd considering the going rate is 15-20% for an agent or manager to take.

These trends really turned me off to the industry because it used to be this tight knit group of people who all knew each other. We all made a shit ton of money, it was fun, and we didn't have to worry too much about STD's because we knew everyone and for the most part the performers were responsible. Now it was different. I didn't feel as safe and companies wanted to make more aggressive type videos since things were becoming so competitive. I was getting to the point where I was over it. It just wasn't fun for me anymore. Thankfully, around this time, webcams rolled out. A lot of porn people started to webcam. Webcamming was really cool because you could do it from the comfort of your own home. You just set up a camera on your computer or use the built-in one, sign up on a site online, and people would pay to watch you masturbate or pay to just talk to you. I also liked webcamming because you could travel and do it from basically anywhere, anytime. The pay was pretty decent too. You could make your own hours and work as little or as much as you wanted. It was also safer because I didn't have to have sex with anyone. During the time I started webcamming, I acted in less and less porn scenes and really just webcammed for the majority of my income.

It was around this time that I decided I was going to get my boobs done (which I totally regret now, but that will be in my next book). While I was recovering from my boob job, I couldn't book regular sex scenes so my agent wanted to book me for my first fetish scene, which was going to be more of an acting job since there was no sex involved, just some mild nudity. I didn't know anything about the fetish world and was really uneducated about most of it. Fetish porn to me is way more difficult to shoot than regular porn because it is not just learning about different fetishes but understanding the psychological aspect of both the submissive and dominant mind. I feel like my time doing fetish porn could be its whole own book, but I will tell you a bit about how I started in fetish porn.

I initially told my agent I didn't want to do the scene, for one, the pay wasn't great and also it was more work as I would have to prep and study for the scene. I got a call back from my agent that same day and the company had offered more money if I agreed to do the shoot. I caved and I said, "Fuck it, I'll do it." I really regretted agreeing to the shoot after I got my call sheet because this company had required that my nails were clear or red and I always painted my nails black at the time. I wasn't going to get my nails done clear or red for what they were paying me so I was annoyed with the company right off the bat. I also never studied for the scene because I never received a script, I was only told that I would be dominant in the video. I would have never agreed to do a submissive scene. The shoot was at night so I brought one of my girlfriend's with me to set because it was a new company and I didn't feel safe going alone. The shoot was also in downtown LA, which is a super sketchy area at night. We pulled up to the address and I had to pull into this dark underground parking garage that was spooky in it's own right. I felt like the moment I stepped out of my car, men in black masks were going to run up and chloroform my friend and I, eat us, and sell our organs or sell us into sex trafficking. I know my mind is twisted but that's what I predicted; I powered through my fears though. The whole situation was odd and scary; as we walked closer to the entrance we were met with this huge metal sliding door that I tried to open but was locked. I knocked on the door and a few moments later it slowly slid open but just a little bit and this man peeked his head out to see who it was. I was puzzled and looked at him thinking I must be in the wrong place or I was walking into a "SAW" movie.

The man instantly recognized me and quickly slid the large metal door all the way open and said very excitedly, "Goddess, please come in." I laughed because he called me

Goddess, but I was relieved I was in the right place and proceeded to walk in. The man quickly shut the door behind us and once the door was shut all these men came out of nowhere and bowed down to me. I was immediately freaked out so I just laughed. I knew it was a fetish shoot, but the shoot hadn't started. I hadn't even filled out paperwork yet or showed my ID. I looked around to see if there was a cameraman shooting or cameras rolling somewhere but I didn't see anything. Everyone was quiet and looking at me so I waited a few seconds thinking maybe I was being pranked and someone would say, "Just kidding, we got you!" But no one said anything. After a long awkward silence I finally said, "Who is in charge here?" I was no longer freaked out, but more annoyed at this point. The man that opened the door quickly came forward and said, "I am Goddess, I mean, Miss Randi." I asked him why everyone was bowing down and where I could change and go over the scene. He quickly apologized and directed me to a private dressing room with my name on it. As I walked through the place towards my dressing room I was looking around and the place was HUGE.

It didn't look very big from outside so I was really surprised. I soon realized it was an UNDERGROUND DUNGEON! It was pretty epic, there were all kinds of crazy torture devices, sex swings, throne chairs, a wall full of spiked paddles, floggers, whips, and even huge human cages hanging from the ceiling. I was in awe. I had done porn and seen some wild stuff in my day, I even had some clients with some odd and interesting fetishes but this was definitely different. I had even been to swingers' parties and secret sex parties but I had never seen an underground DUNGEON before. It was full of new exciting shit! There was something about it that sparked my curiosity. But it also made me nervous because soon I would be filming in this environment and had no clue how to properly use anything I was seeing, let alone dominate another individual and make it come off convincing on camera. I showed up for this shoot sober, and when I wasn't drinking I was mostly soft-spoken, timid, and a bit shy especially around new people. I would be lying if I said this wasn't the most nervous I had been to shoot a scene in years.

The man who was in charge at the shoot was actually also the owner of the fetish company. I found out later that they threw a lot of fetish parties and filmed a lot of fetish videos there. Once I got into my dressing room the man in charge looked at my nails and seemed disappointed that I hadn't got them done. He said to me, "The call sheet said clear or red nails." I wanted to roll my eyes at him and tell him that if he wanted me to do my nails a specific color that he should pay for it because I wasn't getting paid enough for this shoot. Instead I said, "Sorry I didn't have time." It was a blatant lie and I hated lying even about little things, but I was hoping I would make up for it in the scene. I didn't realize how important nail color was for this scene as again I was a total fetish amateur. If I had known how important it was, I definitely would have had my nails done. But I was new, so I didn't know any better. The man in charge, Jeff, went over my scene with me. He told me the men I saw when I first walked in would be worshipping my feet; I would be stomping on them in heels and being mean to them. I thought okay, that doesn't sound too bad. Jeff then pulled out these princess costumes and tiaras and said, "You will wear this." I saw the costumes and thought, I get to wear a princess costume, get worshipped, step on people, and be mean? This sounds AWESOME!

I gladly accepted what to me was a challenge, my first fetish shoot. I got changed and walked out onto set with all the men who Jeff told me were my "slaves." Before I go any further, I need to get one thing straight for anyone reading this that might get confused with the term 'slave.' These men/women in fetish porn are willing and able to be dominated and like being ordered around by another person. It might sound bad but this is part of the fetish world that a lot of people don't understand. When someone doesn't understand something they immediately don't like it or judge it. I was guilty of it myself at first. I was very taken back and a bit disgusted when he called them my slaves, even for the video knowing it was acting. But once I learned more about fetish work, it made much more sense to me. The reason all these 'slaves' bowed down to me when I walked in is because these men were submissive in their personal life as well as 'acting' on camera.

The scene started and I have to admit the foot worshipping thing was weird and made me uncomfortable but I had to remember it was acting and I had to pretend that I enjoyed it. Then it came to the part where I had to step on these guys in my heels and literally walk all over them. I would be putting all my weight on these men in my stiletto heels. This was crazy! I stepped up onto one of the guys and he instantly let out a huge grunt. He was clearly in pain and I had to stop the scene. I instantly got off of him, called cut, and I got down to his level on the ground. I was on my hands and knees and hugged the poor guy and told him how sorry I was and asked if he was okay. He looked at me confused and almost sad that I stopped the scene and he said, "Goddess, please don't stop, I really like it when you hurt me." It almost looked like he was about to cry because I didn't want to keep going. I was shocked as again this was all new to me and I was not used to anyone purposely wanting to have someone inflict pain upon them. I am a people pleaser so knowing that he liked it, surprisingly made me okay with going through with it. This now made sense as to why these 'slaves' were also submissive in real life because no actor would actually be okay enduring the pain these men go through unless they truly enjoyed it. I was starting to pick up on a little bit of the fetish world and how it worked but I was still very green. The cameras started rolling again and I once again stepped up onto the slave in my pointy stiletto heels and he again let out a huge grunt because of the pain. But this time I stayed with all my weight on top of him and slowly started walking on his body. Every step I took he would say in so much pain, "Thank you Goddess." He would say it over and over. Soon I realized after about 20-30 seconds of me walking up and down his chest in my heels this guy had a HUGE erection! He was a true masochist. I couldn't believe it. How could all this pain cause an erection? More and more I was learning at this shoot how different things turn people on. Before I knew it, another submissive came in to lay down before me and beg to be walked on, and one after the other I would walk all over these men for this scene and I got to do it in a tiara. It was becoming really fun and by the end of the scene I was kind of sad it was over because it was so much fun to inflict pain on so many people. Am I a sadist? Maybe I am. But really I just enjoyed doing something that made others happy even if that meant hurting them. Sounds fucked up but it's true. I am a people pleaser.

After the shoot wrapped I was talking to some of the slaves on set because I was so interested in the psychology behind why they got so much pleasure from being abused or in pain. One of them confessed to me that he couldn't get off from regular porn and that he felt like such an outsider and a freak because of what turned him on until he found fetish porn and was able to have a sense of belonging and have his needs met. He opened my eyes so much to something I knew nothing about. I felt sad for him but also happy that he had videos like the one we made that day to entertain and fulfill his needs. As I was leaving the shoot that day, Jeff told me how impressed he was with me during the scenes and that he would love to work with me again. He also paid me double what I was supposed to make that day which made me super happy and very motivated to shoot with him again. He also offered to take me to get my nails done and that was pretty cool too.

The next shoot I ended up doing with Jeff was pretty different than the first. Just when I thought I was getting the hang of the fetish world, Jeff would put me into a scene doing something a little more crazy each time. This time I was ball kicking. Yes, you heard me right. I was kicking guys in the balls as hard as I could. They would lose their breath and keel over in pain after each kick and some would throw up. It was so painful but they all had erections while I was doing it so I would keep going. Jeff would tell me what to say to them. I would talk down to them and humiliate them and the meaner and more abusive I was towards them, the more they liked it. Jeff was smart, he knew I was new to fetish porn so he eased me into it starting with the easy stuff. The next shoot was me tasering Jeff. Jeff was also a submissive, which I later found out. I think the tasering scene was probably one of the craziest scenes I have ever done in my whole life. The shoot was back at the underground dungeon and it was with me and two other girls. We were supposed to taser Jeff with a police taser. It is the hardcore taser that shoots out these two wires and it sticks into their skin and their body goes into convulsions until they end up on the ground. It almost looks like a seizure. None of us had ever used a taser before, so we had no idea how to work the thing. Jeff had to put in all of his information, even his social security number to obtain this taser.

He showed us how to work it in a one-minute lesson. Jeff was on his hands and knees with a collar around his neck, butt naked. We did some dialogue and then I was in charge of tasering him. I turned it on and these red lasers came on as I was pointing it at him. I pressed the trigger button and these two darts shot out at him and stuck into his back. The taser was so forceful that he instantly fell completely to the ground. I freaked out because it looked and felt like I shot him with a real gun! Then he started convulsing on the ground! His body twisted and threw him onto his back and his body kept convulsing. I panicked and as fast as I could, passed the taser to the girl next to me. She couldn't figure out how to turn it off though. I thought we were going to kill him. I didn't want to be the one responsible for accidentally killing a man. He looked like he was in an electrical chair being electrocuted to death. I then grabbed the taser back from her and finally figured out how to turn it off. He laid on the ground limp. I thought he was dead and I was almost in tears. We ran up to him and asked if he was okay. He wasn't. He had never done this before. I don't think he realized how powerful the taser was. I tried pulling the darts out of his back but they were like fish hooks in his skin, they didn't just come out. I had to rip his skin to get them out. We all surrounded him and I asked if he wanted me to call an ambulance and he quickly said, "No, I just need a minute."

I asked one of the girls to get him some water and a towel. He was pretty out of it but after a few minutes he was fine. I was a bit traumatized from that scene and I think he was too. It was scary but it wasn't anything like what I eventually got into which was some DARK shit. The dark side of fetish porn were things like humiliation, cuckolding, putting cigarettes out on human flesh, talking about killing animals, genital mutilation, incest, mom/son seducing, really sick stuff. Like I said, I could write a whole book alone on my time in the fetish world. I've been heavily criticized from a lot of the fetish porn I have done. Some of the racial humiliation and me talking about harming animals videos have been leaked to the general population and people that are uneducated about fetish porn think that I am a racist or that I am sick for talking about harming animals. I understand where they are coming from, but I am vegan and have been for many years and would NEVER even think of harming an animal. I won't even eat them because I love animals so much. I also cry any time I watch a movie with any sort of racism in it and try to educate others on the affects of racism. I feel so sad for racial minorities that have to endure suffering, prejudice, and violence. My personal life is very different from my work life. I know it is really hard for some people to compartmentalize or differentiate porn as acting, but that's what it is, even if the acting is bad. To me, acting is acting whether it's porn, fetish, or mainstream. I show up to set, act out a scene from a script or as instructed by the director, get paid, and move on to the next project. It's as simple as that. You would never think Leonardo DiCaprio is racist in real life because he played one in "Django Unchained". But when you do porn, somehow we are categorized as evil people who are the same as the character we play. I had a script and I was acting just like an actor does in mainstream movies. I would NEVER do the things I did in my fetish porn in my personal life. Even though it was fun for me to do fetish porn, I never enjoyed doing the dark fetish porn even though it was acting. I had a hard time doing it so after a while I refused to do the darker fetishes.

It wasn't until after I was contracted with Jeff's fetish porn company, that he introduced me to the dark fetish world. I was getting booked so much for the same fetish company (Jeff's) that they ended up making me a contract girl. I committed to only working with that company. A contract girl gets paid a set amount per month to shoot a certain amount of scenes for that specific company. Every contract is different but most have a stipulation or clause that states you can't mention how much you get paid or any inside information you hear or come across in the company indefinitely. I am saying everything I can without violating my contract. Part of my contract was that I was to live in a mansion provided by the company that we also used to shoot most of the scenes. The mansion was located in a secluded area in the hills of Encino California called The Mean Girl Manor. I lived there for a while and shot tons of fetish porn while I lived there. Once I had signed this contract, I quit porn and webcamming altogether.

Most of the time, I was having fun doing fetish porn. I was being introduced to all kinds of new fetishes. There is a fetish for EVERYTHING. Brushing hair, cutting hair, chewing gum, you name it, someone is getting off to it. When we threw fetish parties at the MGM (Mean Girl Manor) I met even more men that wanted to take me on shopping sprees, take me and my friends to get our nails done, take us to nice dinners, and some even offered to pay for me to go on trips. It was really awesome. The type of submissive that got off on us spending their money are also sometimes known as cash cows, money slaves, or pay pigs. Essentially, they are into financial domination. The slaves who wanted to pay for trips for me to go on were in to cuckolding. Cuckolding is when a guy gets off to a woman being unfaithful. The cucks wanting to pay for trips were into financial domination and cuckolding together.

During this time, I was loving work but I was also getting lonely. I was longing for a normal relationship since my world was full of crazy fantasies and chaos that most would find unrealistic. I wanted to settle down with someone. I had no clue who would be normal enough to want to settle down with someone like me though. When I first started porn, I was told to start saving up a bunch of footage to create a website of all this porn I had shot myself with other performers for free so that I could put it on a website and have people pay membership fees. It is hard to have a regular job after doing porn and a website helps. I'd been smart with my money at this point and I had more than enough footage to retire on. Or so I thought. I figured I could go to nursing school and do that part time but also have money coming in just in case I got fired for being an ex-porn star. But now, all of the porn I had shot was a complete waste because of all the free porn online. No one wanted to pay for it now. I no longer had the opportunity to make the money like I could have previously. I even tried having companies in the past run my websites but they all screwed me over and just took all the money. I was taken advantage of multiple times in the past with trying to start my own website. I gave up on that. I still have those videos and I am just sitting on them now. I did however save a decent amount of money from my time in porn. But unfortunately, I would still need to work and I wouldn't be able to retire at the age I planned. So I kept doing my fetish work.

Some of my friends had convinced me to start dating online and I was super skeptical because for one I thought it was weird to meet someone online and two, I was a porn star who now did fetish porn and most people would not want to date someone like that, let alone get serious with them. I eventually went for it as I really had nothing to lose. My heart had been broken so many times and I was SUPER jaded with guys from all the escorting I had done and previous relationships that broke my soul. I decided I was going to try one last time at a relationship and if it didn't work this time, then I was really going to give up for good. I got on my computer and signed myself up online to meet guys. Within hours I had an overwhelming amount of messages in my inbox of people wanting to meet up. It was kind of exciting but I didn't actually want to meet these people in real life. I just liked the idea of them wanting to date me. I figured if people found out who I was behind that girl in the picture they would soon be uninterested. I didn't want it to get to that point.

Out of hundreds of messages I read through in the next few days, there were two guys I decided I would meet. One of the guys was a therapist and I was so nervous to meet up that I ended up getting drunk just to meet him. I know it's ridiculous but I was just so scared of being hurt again and drinking was the only way I knew how to deal with my feelings temporarily. I met him at a restaurant and he was super hot but really weird. We had some interesting conversations and even though he was really good-looking and had a decent job, I wasn't really into him. I also think he knew who I was and just wanted to meet me. I was right because by the end of the night I told him that I used to do porn and he said he already knew that and then he wanted to ask me a million questions about why I got into it and I felt like I was in a therapy session but for his own satisfaction and curiosity, not to actually help me in anyway. He was a bit odd for me so I didn't end up seeing him again.

The second date I ended up going on was with a firefighter. I met up with him at a coffee shop and he was also very good-looking but also super religious and during our meeting, we realized we weren't a good fit but could totally be friends. He was super sweet but we never ended up talking again. But hey, I tried and that was all I could do. I was done trying to find someone even though I was really lonely. It was when I felt like giving up that I kept getting a message from this same guy that I wasn't really interested in. He wasn't that great looking and I need to find someone attractive to be able to date them. I know I am superficial in that sense, but it is what it is. Anyway, I finally just gave the guy my number. We texted a bit but I never met up with him because I really didn't want to. Almost a month went by and the guy was so persistent on messaging me to meet up. I finally, out of annoyance, ended up agreeing to meet this guy. I figured it would be like all the rest of my meetings with these guys online, but this night was different. Something happened to me that night that would change my life forever.

To be continued…

Thank you so much for reading my second book. In my third book I will talk about how I got out of the porn and fetish industry and how I started doing YouTube and social media full-time. I will talk about how I met my husband, details about why we no longer speak to or have a relationship with my husband's side of the family, getting married which involved a theft, police reports, lawyers, and restraining orders, more YouTube drama, me almost dying (again), years of my infertility struggles, IUI and IVF procedures, giving birth to my miracle baby and much more. As of this books publication date I'm currently doing YouTube and social media full-time and you can join me and the Rose Family and keep up to date by checking out and following the links below. Thank you again for all your love and support it means more to me than you will ever know! I can't tell you how special it is to me that you love and accept me for who I am no matter my past. I have had a lot of people no longer want to be friends with me once finding out about my past so it really means a lot that you are still here and supporting me, growing with me, and being a part of the best most supportive family online, The Rosefam. I am sending you all my love and all my positive energy! MUAH! xoxo

My First Book: https://amzn.to/2KBRy5Q
Main YouTube Channel: www.youtube.com/ChannonRose1
Vlog YouTube Channel: www.youtube.com/channonrosevlogs
Beauty YouTube Channel: https://bit.ly/2jZOmqM
Instagram: www.instagram.com/channonrose/
Twitter: www.twitter.com/ChannonRose

Love, Channon Rose
xoxo

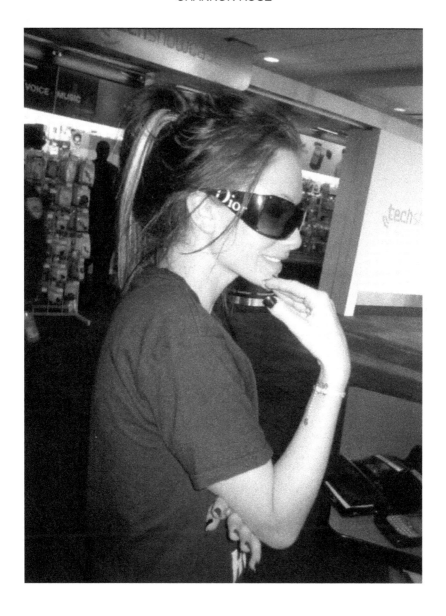

CPSIA information can be obtained
at www.ICGtesting.com
Printed in the USA
LVHW081321150821
695353LV00011B/533

9 781087 978451